SIBLING RELATIONSHIPS IN STEP-FAMILIES
A Sociological Study

SIBLING RELATIONSHIPS IN STEP-FAMILIES
A Sociological Study

Monique Diderich

With a Foreword by
Veronica Manlow

The Edwin Mellen Press
Lewiston•Queenston•Lampeter

Library of Congress Cataloging-in-Publication Data

Diderich, Monique.
    Sibling relationships in step-families : a sociological study / Monique Diderich ; with a foreword by Veronica Manlow.
        p. cm.
    Includes bibliographical references and index.
    ISBN-13: 978-0-7734-4971-8
    ISBN-10: 0-7734-4971-X
    1. Stepchildren--Family relationships--United States. 2. Brothers and sisters--United States. 3. Stepfamilies--United States. I. Title.
HQ777.7.D53 2008
306.8750973--dc22
                                            2008041771

hors série.

A CIP catalog record for this book is available from the British Library.

Front Cover Illustration: Thaddeus Kellstadt

Copyright © 2008 Monique Diderich

All rights reserved. For information contact

>   The Edwin Mellen Press   The Edwin Mellen Press
>   Box 450   Box 67
>   Lewiston, New York   Queenston, Ontario
>   USA 14092-0450   CANADA L0S 1L0

>   The Edwin Mellen Press, Ltd.
>   Lampeter, Ceredigion, Wales
>   UNITED KINGDOM SA48 8LT

Printed in the United States of America

For my siblings: Jolande, Cassandra, and Christian

TABLE OF CONTENTS

Foreword by Veronica Manlow   i

Acknowledgements   iii

Chapter One:	**American Families**	3
	American Family Structure	4
	Remarried Families	5
	Methodology	10
	Implications	12
Chapter Two:	**Classical and Contemporary Views on Marriage**	15
	Classical Views on Marriage and Family	15
	Contemporary Views: Twentieth Century Theories	20
	Structural-functionalists	20
	Social Exchange and Social Comparison Theories	22
	Evolutionary Theories and Views about Sexuality	28
	Feminist Perspectives	29
	Summary	37

Chapter Three:	**Sibling Relationships**	**39**
	Sibling Differentiation	40
	Family Constellation and Parental Factors	42
	Children's Perspectives	47
	Quality of Sibling Relationships	52
	Sibling Solidarity and Rivalry across Cultures	55
	Sibling Relationships after Divorce and Remarriage	58
	Summary	61
Chapter Four:	**Methods of Sociological Inquiry**	**65**
	Feminist Critiques on Methods of Sociological Inquiry	66
	Qualitative Research	68
	Blended Family Workshops	72
	Family of Orientation Project	74
	Quantitative Research	75
	General Social Survey	77
Chapter Five:	**Results**	**79**
	Findings from the Blended Family Workshops	79
	Findings from the Family of Orientation Project	87
	Family	89
	Siblings in Remarried Families	91
	Full Siblings	97
	Full Siblings and Half Siblings	101
	Favorite Sibling and Type of Solidarity	102
	Findings from the 1994 General Social Survey	105
	Findings from the 1986 and 2002 General Social Survey	114
	Limitations	120

Chapter Six:	**Conclusion and Discussion**	**123**
	Findings	123
	Hypotheses	131
	Conclusion and Implications	133

References	**139**
Index	**155**

List of Tables

Table 1	Type of Family	88
Table 2	Remarried Family and Preferred Sibling	92
Table 3	Preference and Number of Full Siblings Present	94
Table 4	Favorite Sibling and Type of Solidarity	103
Table 5	Children and Parent's Relatedness	106
Table 6	Number of Siblings and Genetic Relatedness	107
Table 7	Sibling Picked and Genetic Relatedness	108
Table 8	Siblings and Relationship	109
Table 9	Socializing with Sibling	110
Table 10	Number of Siblings, Type of Sibling and Frequency of Socialization	111
Table 11	Background Variables GSS 1986, 1994, and 2002	114
Table 12	Functional Solidarity in Percentages	115
Table 13	Affectual Solidarity in Percentages	117
Table 14	Associational Solidarity in Percentages	118

FOREWORD
Contemporary Families

In this interesting book, sociologist Monique Diderich examines stepfamilies and in particular the dynamics that shape sibling relationships (full siblings, half siblings and step siblings) in the United States, a country that has the world's highest rate of divorce and remarriage.

Families matter. We are born into a family unit and we share a significant part of our formal and our personal lives with our family members. For some family members we have warm feelings, for others we could care less. We don't choose our family, yet we have to get along with individual family members during holidays and special occasions, and indeed on a daily basis. For some of us, cheerful occasions are much looked forward to; while others dread family events and cannot suppress disdain or outright animosity.

These family dynamics – as difficult as they may seem – are considered relatively normal in traditional nuclear families. Everyone who has had the privilege of organizing an event where family members are present does so with individual preferences and personalities of their kin in mind. Not to do so would constitute arguments and strife and a possible ruined family gathering. Nevertheless, in our society, the traditional nuclear family is viewed as the 'ideal type' of family. Divorced families, and blended families or stepfamilies, are also labeled as 'broken' and 'reconstituted' families.

Dr. Diderich, a Dutch native, can be considered an 'outsider looking in'. Her educational and personal background, as well as her decade long residency in the United States, give her the benefit of an objective scholarly view since she witnessed Americans' sincere commitment to family, whether they are part of single parent families, nuclear families, divorced families, extended families, or stepfamilies.

The author bases her findings on three separate studies: participant observation in a series of Blended Family Workshops, reflections of 215 young adults about their family of orientation as articulated in a 'Family of Orientation' assignment, and an examination of three large secondary data sets. Based on her research, she gives tips and provides tools for everyone who is part of a stepfamily, whether as a new stepparent or as an adult who has grown up in a stepfamily. Monique Diderich also demonstrates that children of divorce are resilient and can cope with their parents' divorce and become healthy adults. Furthermore, her message is that stepfamilies can overcome hurdles and become as 'normal' as traditional nuclear families where adults are, despite strife and sometimes enmity, also very loving of family in general and siblings in particular.

In our society, where family values supposedly are high on politicians' agendas, we do not have generous paid vacations or enough leisure to spend time with family. Our holidays are always on Mondays (with a few exceptions) as to allow for three day weekends. Americans work one month per year more compared to their European counterparts. Time spent at work cannot be spent with family. Monique Diderich offers some solutions for spending more time with family, and provides guidance for parents who want to foster cohesion and solidarity among their offspring, because family and families do matter.

Veronica Manlow, Ph.D.
Assistant Professor of Sociology
Department of Economics, Brooklyn College

ACKNOWLEDGEMENTS

A research study is never the fruit of the labor of just one person. I owe thanks to colleagues, friends, and the people who took part in this study. First and foremost, I would like to thank Dr. Donald Carns, Dr. David Dickens, Dr. William Jankowiak and Dr. Ronald Smith for their guidance, advice and stimulating intellectual conversations during the stages of this project.

The participants in the Blended Families Workshops provided useful insights into the topic of this study; I thank them for their openness about their family life. Sarah Beers and Jan Bialecki were helpful by allowing me to participate in these workshops. I thank Dr. David Damore, who was ICPSR's local representative, for his help in obtaining the General Social Survey data sets.

I had many interesting conversations with my friends and colleagues in the Sociology Department at the University of Nevada Las Vegas and would like to especially acknowledge the following persons: Barb Brents, Andrea Fontana, Kathy Gilpatrick, Bill Goldberg, Simon Gottschalk, Kate Hausbeck, Catherine Moorhead, Kathy Nelson, Robert Parker and Dmitri Shalin.

Dr. Robert Perinbanayagam at Hunter College in New York encouraged me to get this study published with the Edwin Mellen Press and I thank him for his advice and encouragement. Throughout the years, I had many thought provoking conversations about marriage and family with Dr. Veronica Manlow. A special thanks to her for agreeing to write the foreword to this book.

Dr. Victoria Hilkevitch Bedford and Dr. Karla Hackstaff carefully scrutinized the entire manuscript. I thank them for their advice, comments and help with the successful completion. This book is better because of their combined expertise pertaining to the subject matter.

SIBLING RELATIONSHIPS IN STEP-FAMILIES
A Sociological Study

CHAPTER ONE
American Families

This book focuses on marriage and the family, and in particular on remarried families and the siblings who become part of those families. The initial idea for this research project originated in 1998 when I moved from The Netherlands to the Unites States, and was confronted with the overwhelming impact of divorce and remarriage on the individuals within those family constellations: parents and their offspring. Since divorce and one or multiple remarriages are common in this country, I became intrigued with the complexity of American family life, and started conducting research pertaining to this topic.

I was equally puzzled by Americans' emphasis on dating and marriage. In my culture, the norm was to get an education first and to postpone marriage, which was advocated by the Dutch government in the 1980s. It was considered 'normal' for any young Dutch adult to live by themselves or to live together in a domestic partnership. Marriage was, at that time, not seen as an ideal that my generation pursued and in fact, many of my friends did not marry or eventually married their live-in boyfriend or girlfriend when they decided to start a family. I realized soon that family structure and cultural concepts pertaining to marriage and family are very different in the United States.

This study addresses today's reality that, in the United States, about half of all first marriages eventually dissolve, which is the world's highest divorce rate, and that the majority of divorced people remarry, thus creating a blended type of family consisting of a variety of individuals who may or may not be blood relatives; who may or may not get along with each other; who face problems in establishing family bonds; who face problems with parenting their (step)children, and the impact of these children on the success or failure of their (step) parents' marriage. I am particularly interested in the problems and issues that arise in remarried families, in the level of cohesion within remarried families, and in the level of cohesion and solidarity among blended sibling groups.

American Family Structure

In recent decades, the structure of the American family has changed considerably. The traditional nuclear family, organized around husband, wife and their biological offspring, is no longer the dominant family form. Bohannan and Erickson (1978) noted in the 1970s that an estimated half of the couples married in that decade would eventually divorce. It was also estimated that the majority of divorced people would eventually remarry. Consequently, many children are raised in blended households or stepfamilies. In 1980, there was already a high incidence of stepfamilies in the United States: 25 million stepparents (residential and non-residential) and 6.5 million children living in stepfamily households (Skeen, Robinson and Flake-Hobson 1984). In 1995, nearly one million marriages ended in divorce and they involved an estimated number of almost two million children (U.S. Bureau of the Census 1997). Currently, as indicated by Kreider and Fields (2001), in the United States, approximately 1.2 million couples divorce each year. Half of those people who divorce remarry within three years. In fact, the interval between marriage and divorce, and divorce and remarriage is seven and three years respectively (Ihinger-Tallman and Pasley 1987). Among other industrialized countries, England has the second highest divorce rate, and 33 percent of all marriages there are remarriages for one or both partners (Simpson 1998).

In the United States, 40 percent of marriages are remarriages for one or both of the newlyweds. The majority of divorced people (61 percent) remarry other divorcees (Ganong and Coleman 1994). Five out of six divorced men remarry and three out of four divorced women remarry (Emery 1988). About half of all

American school age children are not raised in a family where both biological parents are present (ERS Staff Report 1995). In 2006, 67 percent of children between the ages of 0 and 17 lived with two married parents. Yet, the definition 'living with two married parents' includes children who live with a biological, adoptive and/or step parent (Federal Interagency Forum on Child and Family Statistics 2007).

Judith Stacey, who analyzes the postmodern family, notes a diversity of contemporary kinship relations: "No longer is there a single culturally dominant family pattern..." ([1996] 1999:647). However, the predominant view of the postmodern family is the two-earner, heterosexual married couple with children. The postmodern family stands for a variety of contemporary family cultures such as families of color, single parent families, same-sex couples, extended families, and remarried families (Stacey [1996] 1999). In fact, the remarried family is projected to be the dominant family form in the United States by the census year 2010 (Berger 1998).

Remarried Families

Remarried families are also known as blended families, reconstituted families, stepfamilies and bi-nuclear families. They are families that have been formed after the death of or divorce from a previous spouse and include a child or children from one or several previous marriages.

Historically, remarriages were common after the death of a spouse, and occurred because of instrumental motives such as a need for economic resources or childcare and household needs (i.e., the need for a wife and homemaker to raise the already present children). A popular depiction was a 1970s television series *The Brady Bunch,* in which a widower with three male children married a widow with three daughters. This 'traditional remarried family' was depicted as a happy family. Such families were originally portrayed as families without problems.

A remarriage after the death of a spouse is different from a remarriage after a divorce. A widower or widow may have fond and loving memories about the deceased spouse, whereas a divorced person may try to establish a cordial relationship with the ex-spouse for the sake of their children, yet, may even feel bitter about the divorce.

Blended families can have a simple family structure but may also be more complex (e.g., Berger 1998). A widow with children, who are each other's full siblings, who marries a childless man is an example of a simple blended family structure. The children would only have to adjust to their stepfather and vice versa (e.g., Bohannan and Erickson 1978; Marsiglio 2004; Marsiglio and Hinojosa 2007).

A more complex situation is a widow with children who marries a widower with children. The children would have to adjust to their stepsiblings and to their stepmother or stepfather. This family structure reflects the aforementioned *Brady Bunch*. The family structure becomes more complex when a divorced person with children marries someone who also has children. These families may have a variety of family members: stepparents, stepsiblings, and possibly half siblings. Stepsiblings do not share biological parents: there is no genetic relatedness. Half siblings share only one biological parent. Not only do members of these households have to establish parent-child relationships and sibling relationships with each other, they may have to deal with more complex situations, such as a co-parent in joint custody situations and/or one or more non-residential biological parents with visitation rights.

Research on remarried families has addressed the quality of stepparent-child interaction, the spousal relationship and spouses' satisfaction with their current marriage, ignoring however, sibling interaction in blended sibling groups (e.g., Baxter, Braithwaite, Bryant and Wagner 2004; Bohannan and Erickson 1978; Cherlin 1978; Cherlin 1983; Ihinger-Tallman 1987b; Ihinger-Tallman 1988; Skeen et al. 1984.)

The debate in the scholarly literature has revolved around whether divorce is positive or negative and how it affects children (e.g., Popenoe 1996). At the opposite ends of this debate are scholars affiliated with the Council on Contemporary Families who have a more positive stance on divorce and remarriage, and scholars affiliated with the Institute for American Values (e.g., Glenn 1997).

Some scholars argue that divorce can have positive effects (e.g., Applewhite 1997; Hetherington and Kelly 2002; Kurz 1995). Wallerstein, in her landmark study, points out that divorce generates winners and losers, and that, above all, "the effects of divorce are often long-lasting". She further notes that "Children are especially affected because divorce occurs during their formative years" (Wallerstein and Blakeslee 1990: 297-298). Other scholars, such as Constance Ahrons (2004), suggest that divorce is not necessarily detrimental and that remarried families can live harmonious lives with kinship ties to previous kin (i.e., a former mother-in-law, an ex-spouse). Opponents of divorce focus on results suggesting that, contrary to popular beliefs, divorce does not make people happier, as articulated by scholars affiliated with the aforementioned Institute for American Values (Waite, Browning, Doherty, Gallagher, Luo, and Stanley 2002). Ergo, their message is that people may as well stay married. These scholars also point to the higher incidence of crime, drug use, alcohol use, sex at an earlier age, and teenage pregnancies among children from divorced households.

In the 1970s, stepfamilies were portrayed in a negative manner, and books pertaining to these families "exposed a "doomsday mentality"" (Pasley and Ihinger-Tallman 1985:532). However, the depiction of the nuclear family as the happy and the ideal family in which to raise children is a romanticized picture, according to historian Stephanie Coontz who debunked myths about the traditional nuclear family, notably in her books *The Way We Never Were* and *The Way We Really Are* (1992; 1997).

Children are affected by the divorce and remarriage of their parents in many ways (e.g., Furstenberg and Teitler 1994). They have to cope with the absence of the non-residential parent, and they may have to deal with a loss in economic resources, as women and children are the ones who generally lose financially in divorces (Ganong and Coleman 1994). It is estimated that divorce leads to a 27 percent decrease in women's standard of living (Peterson 1996). As a consequence of divorce, children may move out of their neighborhoods to poorer neighborhoods, thereby severing ties with friends, schools and other community-based institutions. For them, remarriage is the fastest route out of poverty or a lower standard of living (South, Crowder, and Trent 1998).

Researchers have examined the reasons behind divorce while tying changes in the family to changes in contemporary society (e.g., Coontz; 2000; 2005; Hackstaff 1999; Rubin 1996). Individuals do get married but it is no longer 'until death do us part'. Marriages dissolve and people remarry. Marriage dissolution is an example of a general trend in contemporary American society, which is dominated by short-term relationships, both in employment situations and in friendships, as well as in family situations (Rubin 1996). Thus, we consume and dispose of marriages in the same fashion as we do with numerous other elements in our society.

Boteach (2008) suggests that societal pressures, and in particular advanced capitalism with its focus on finances and financial gain, are detrimental to American families. Others explain divorce in terms of either structural changes in society, such as no-fault divorce laws which redefined marriage as a time limited arrangement, women's increasing economic independence, the lack of family friendly policies in work organizations, or individual characteristics such as an increase in self-centeredness, and a desire for equality in marriage (e.g., Ball and Kivisto 2006; Hackstaff 1999; Harris 2000; Rogers 2004). However, as Hackstaff notes, "the rise of divorce disempowers married women by serving as a cautionary tale and reinforcing submission in marriage" (1999:178).

Lasch (1975) laments the demise of the family as a safe haven, whereas Hochschild (1997; 1999) makes the argument that our workplace has taken over that function in a society where a fragmented family no longer functions as the haven we yearn for.

The struggles and challenges for remarried families are real. They are fragile, and in the first years every individual involved needs to adjust to his or her new family (e.g., Spanier and Furstenberg 1987). Family cohesion needs to be negotiated as well as relationships with ex-spouses, relationships with extended former kin, stepparent child relationships, and relationships between the children, whether they are full, half or step siblings. Indeed, the failure rate of remarriages is higher than for first marriages and scholars suggest that how well the children get along is one of the main factors in the success or failure of the remarriage. Emery (1988) found evidence that the presence of stepchildren is related to an increased likelihood of divorce in remarriages and would account for the high divorce rate of sixty percent in second marriages. Recently, Teachman (2008) discovered an increased risk of marital dissolution in second marriages where women had children from a previous marriage (mother-stepfather households). Further, when stepsibling relationships are good, there is a positive influence on "the total family integration" (Duberman 1973:291).

Divorce and remarriage lead to an extension of family ties and kinship confusion: who is included in the family and who is not? In particular, children are confused about kinship. Are stepsiblings from their father's second marriage that also dissolved still regarded as kin? Is their stepmother's sister their step aunt? Are the parents of your stepmother your step grandparents? What about the grandparents of your half sister? Are they also included in your family? What about the stepsiblings acquired through mother's second marriage? Anthropologist Simpson terms this diffusion of kinship the "unclear family" (1998:2). Interestingly, among low socioeconomic level families, divorce means that a former spouse's siblings are no longer recognized as kin although they technically remain offspring's aunt or uncle (Farber 1973; Rosenberg and Anspach 1973).

Studies on sibling solidarity, with a few exceptions (e.g., Brody, Stoneman, Smith and Gibson 1999), primarily addressed siblings in white nuclear families. We know from the existing body of literature on full siblings that, through differential treatment, parents can shape the relationship between their children.

Whenever family solidarity in remarried families was the focus of research, these studies primarily addressed the relationship between adult children and their step-parent(s), and adult children with their siblings in comparison with intact traditional nuclear families. Results indicate that adults from intact families felt closer toward all their siblings than adults who were raised in remarried families (Pulakos 1990). Thus, it appears that family cohesion and sibling solidarity in remarried families tend to be weaker than in traditional nuclear families.

When stepfamilies are formed, its family members experience ambivalence, in particular about establishing and maintaining boundaries: "Between step-relations there is a tension between getting close and staying distant in order to remain loyal to a biological parent or child" (Galvin, Bylund and Brommel 2004:72). The concept of ambivalence has two components. Structural ambivalence stems from an individual's location in the social structure (within the family). Psychological ambivalence refers to sentiments experienced by individuals when faced with structural ambivalence (Bengtson, Giarrusso, Mabry, and Silverstein 2002; Luescher 2002).

Methodology

This study focuses solely on families that consist of partners married to each other, and thus excludes cohabiting partners, since the literature suggests that, in the United States, there are fewer ties and less commitment in families where partners have not married. Given the research topic, I concentrate on remarried families, which include children from previous marriages and thus include some type of constellation of full siblings, stepsiblings and/or half siblings.

Scholars have critiqued prior research pertaining to families, in particular the over emphasis on a positivist discourse (e.g., Allen 2000; Fox and Murray 2000). I therefore employ a triangulation of qualitative and quantitative methods (see chapter four for a complete description of the research methods).

As a first step, I sought participation in a series of 'Blended Family Workshops' in order to gain a better understanding of the initial problems and issues that arise in newly formed remarried families. The second part of this research study includes a 'Family of Orientation' assignment in which college students reflect upon the family in which they were raised. As such, this part of the research project generates rich data about a variety of family constellations, including traditional nuclear families and remarried families, the ties among family members, and feelings about their full siblings, half siblings, and step siblings who are or who are not considered part of those families.

The last part of the study includes the analyses of a secondary dataset: the General Social Survey. I examined the 1986, 1994 and 2002 waves of the General Social Survey regarding sibling solidarity and family cohesion.

The concept of solidarity is developed by Bengtson and Roberts (1991) and Silverstein and Bengtson (1997). They constructed a scale pertaining to different types of indicators of solidarity. Functional solidarity depicts the degree of helping and exchange of resources (e.g., financial assistance). Associational solidarity is measured by the occurrence of interaction and participation in shared activities. Affectual solidarity is the equivalent of emotional closeness. Normative solidarity is based on the presence of an ideology that emphasizes promoting family cohesion within the remarried family.

William Jankowiak and I already modified and adapted these solidarity scales in a study pertaining to sibling solidarity in polygamous families in the United States. We found evidence that despite an ideology that fosters a harmonious family, siblings tend to display more solidarity toward their full siblings than toward their half siblings. In this polygamous community, siblings, through the guidance of their birthmother, tend to cluster around their birthmother's unit. Further, solidarity between siblings is influenced by age and gender. Children of the same sex who are close in age have a higher degree of solidarity than children who are not close in age and who are of the opposite sex, regardless of genetic relatedness (Jankowiak and Diderich 2000).

Mothers usually get custody of their children (in more than 73 percent of divorce cases in which custody was awarded, 16 percent are given joint custody (Clarke 1995)), and thus those children continue to reside with them in the years following the divorce and during the years of the possible remarriage. Unfortunately, the National Center for Health Statistics suspended collection of detailed data about custody arrangements as from January 1996 and thus it is no longer reported in the National Vital Statistics Reports. However, there are data about the type of households in which children reside. In 2004, the majority of children who live in remarried families reside in households with their mother and stepfather (as opposed to father-stepmother households). In one parent households, the majority of children live with their mother (23 percent) and five percent live with their father. However, these statistics may include a cohabiting partner (Federal Interagency Forum on Child and Family Statistics 2007).

Both the 'Family of Orientation' assignment and the General Social Survey prove useful in addressing the following questions: What is the level of functional solidarity among siblings?; What is the level of associational solidarity among siblings?; What is the level of affectual solidarity among siblings?; What is the level of normative solidarity within the remarried family?

Implications

This study examines family ties and sibling relationships (full siblings, half siblings and stepsiblings) in remarried families, and thus expands our knowledge of half sibling and stepsibling solidarity. The study offers a better understanding of remarried families and the challenges they face, and gains useful insights into people's personal remarried family life. The strength of this study stems from two sources: it employs a variety of research methods (qualitative and quantitative); and it provides a perspective on remarried families from individuals at different stages in the life course, in particular young adults (Family of Orientation), older adults (General Social Survey datasets) and adults in a newly formed remarried family (Blended Family Workshops).

This book addresses an important gap in the scholarly literature: postmodern remarried families and their blended sibling groups, and as such it is a valuable contribution to the scholarly debate within the larger academic community. In addition, this study offers useful insights for those who want to make a success of their remarriage, which may thereby lower the rate of divorce in remarriages. Individuals, who have been raised in a remarried family type, may gain valuable information that enhances their understanding of their own family life, both in their past and in their present. This study may thus empower people in a blended family of orientation and/or in a blended family of procreation.

Further, the results of this study are useful for professionals who deal with remarried families, such as counselors and child psychologists. Lastly, the contents of this book may be fruitful for policymakers pertaining to families. In particular, chapter six may provide them with argumentation to expand the Family and Medical Leave Act. Families are the basic unit for socialization of individuals. Well-integrated families generally produce well-integrated individuals.

CHAPTER TWO

Classical and Contemporary Views on Marriage

Within sociology there are many different perspectives on marriage and the family. Eighteenth, nineteenth, and early twentieth century European scholars focus on evolution, function, economics, and group dynamics within the family. They describe different aspects of marriage and the family. This chapter provides an in-depth overview of classical sociological perspectives on the family as well as contemporary views ranging the gamut from exchange theories to feminist theories. The chapter also addresses the historical background of family formation, and frames remarried families in their historical and theoretical sociological context.

Classical Views on Marriage and Family

Engels [1884, 1892] (1942) argues that marriage arrangements have evolved through the centuries, and that private property (or the absence thereof) has been the main criterion leading to the formation of the nuclear family consisting of husband, wife, and their biological children. The monogamous family has not always been the dominant family form but was preceded by different types of family constellations. Engels acknowledges community or group marriages during so-called primitive history, which were characterized by unrestricted sexual freedom. Descent could therefore only be proven on the mother's side and thus only the female line is recognized for inheritance purposes, a phenomenon coined *Mutterrecht* or Mother Right. Promiscuous sexual relations were not considered extramarital affairs because technically speaking sexual intercourse took place with the partners in the group marriage. Special types of group marriages are polyandrous arrangements, in which one wife shares several men, usually brothers, and polygamous marriages in which one man is married to several wives.

Throughout human history, the family developed from group marriages (inclusion of brother-sister marriages in the consanguine family type and exclusion of parent-child marriages) to the punaluan family (exclusion of brother-sister and cousin-cousin marriages). The typical punaluan family consisted of a number of brothers married to a number of sisters and evolved into the pairing family (exclusion of females' sexual promiscuity) and finally evolved into the monogamous family. Whereas men and women were more equal in the consanguine and punaluan family, male dominance became a factor in the pairing family and monogamous family. The purpose of the latter was to produce offspring of undisputed paternity, and thus legitimate heirs to their father's property. Moreover, in these types of families only the husband was allowed to dissolve the marriage and engage in sexual intercourse with females other than his wife. Husband's sexual freedom was labeled 'hetaerism'. A wife's promiscuity was perceived as adultery.

It is in the early monogamous family where the first division of labor and economic oppression took place: women became confined to household duties and child-rearing activities. The wife became the head servant within the patriarchal monogamous family. As Engels states it: "The modern individual family is founded on the domestic slavery of the wife" ([1884, 1892] 1942:65). Monogamy, on the part of the female, was required in order to ensure that a man's wealth was transferred to his legitimate offspring.

In sum, Friedrich Engels describes a development from matriarchal communistic families, such as the consanguine and punaluan family in which children can only inherit from their mother, to patriarchal household communities such as the pairing family, and the modern isolated family (or nuclear family) along the lines of paternity certainty and acquisition of private property. Within the nuclear family, the husband was the dominant force because he owned the property and restricted his wife to domestic labor.

Freud ([1930] 1961:46) explains the origins of the family not in terms of property ownership but in terms of the satisfaction of sexual and economic needs. Man's urge for sex leads him to find a female and keep her as his helper. Once there are offspring, the woman needs to stay with the stronger male for the protection he can give her and her children. Freud defines love in terms of sex since it is a "relation between a man and a woman whose genital needs have led them to found a family" (Freud, [1930] 1961:49). Primitive man, as a savage beast, met two of his needs by the acquisition of a female: unlimited access to fulfill his sexual needs and labor to meet his economic needs. Freud views the power of love and the compulsion to work as the basis of our communal life. Working together is not enough to keep people together. It is the Eros (or sex) instinct that motivates human individuals to create units such as families, communities and nations, according to Freud.

George Simmel offers a micro-sociological approach to the family and focuses on group dynamics. The smallest group consists of interaction between two people, such as a husband and wife. In the dyad, the two participants, husband and wife, share a similar purpose: to sustain the marriage and the pair bond. Although, according to Simmel, marriage is an institution that destroys the intimate meaning of erotic life, marriage is also "valuable and sacred in itself" (Simmel in Wolff 1950:129). Marriage is very personal and has an individual character although it is "socially regulated and historically transmitted" (Simmel in Wolf 1950:130). A marriage is a special form of a dyad in which the partners are very close and intimate. In intimate relationships, both closeness (e.g., sharing of information and feelings) and distance (e.g., not revealing everything about oneself) are required. In contrast to friendships, "Marriage, essentially, allows only acceptance or rejection, but not modification" (1950:130). A group of two individuals radically changes when a third individual, in this case a child, is added. The dyad expands into a triad and two separate units within this triad emerge: the parental unit and the child unit. The third party strengthens the parental unit because there is a common goal to provide for the child until it reaches maturity. Simmel observes that in the nineteenth and early twentieth century women lacked objective cultural accomplishments and attributes this to the division of labor. Women are nevertheless important as they have "a creative impact on a grand scale: the home and the influence of women upon men" (Simmel 1984:90).

Cooley (1961), in discussing the social self, states that the family is a primary group characterized by intimacy, face-to-face interaction and cooperation. The family as a social unit serves to socialize the nature and ideals of its members. Human nature is not present at birth; we acquire it through fellowship, first within the family and then within secondary groups.

Auguste Comte, acknowledged as 'the father of sociology' because he made up the term sociology, views the division of labor in the family as a natural fact and as a social fact. The family is a "true social unit" (1975:267) where children should be educated in cooperative behavior. Further, family life is "the school of social life, both for obedience and command" (1975:270). Due to the different psychological make up of the sexes, a woman's natural place is in the domestic sphere. According to Comte, women are not fit for reasoning and abstract thinking, whereas they are superior in sensibility, sympathy and sociability. Therefore, it is within the family that women must "modify...the general direction necessarily originated by the cold and rough reason that is distinctive of man" (1975:269). Comte views the division of labor between men (public sphere) and women (domestic sphere) as perfectly natural. A woman's place is in the family where she performs household duties and child rearing activities.

Durkheim focuses on the functions of the family and points out that integration in the family is an essential component to prevent loneliness, anomie and ultimately suicide. His research showed that suicide is three times more frequent among bachelors than among married people. Married people with children are even more strongly attached to life. The family connects people to life "to the extent that familial society is more or less cohesive, tightly knit and strong, man is more or less strongly attached to life" (Giddens 1972:113). In *Suicide*, Durkheim phrases the impact of family breakdown and divorce on anomie and suicide rates: "The state of conjugal anomy, produced by the institution of divorce, thus explains the parallel development of divorces and suicides (Durkheim [1897] 1951:273).

Unlike Engels, Durkheim views the division of labor between husband and wife as potentially positive because it creates interdependency and organic solidarity. Therefore, relationships are strengthened. However, he notes that family life is undermined by industrialization since man has to work outside the home and is thus separated from his family during the time he spends at work.

Max Weber views marriage as an economic arrangement that provides security for the wife and inheritance for the child(ren). He further notes that it legitimizes the erotic realm. Weber writes:

> The erotic relation seems to offer the unsurpassable peak of the fulfillment of the request for love in the direct fusion of the souls of one to the other. This boundless giving of oneself is as radical as possible in its opposition to all functionality, rationality, and generality (Weber in Gerth and C. Wright Mills 1958:347).

Marriage also serves to regulate eroticism since there is a tension between religion and animalistic sex. "Inner-worldly and rational asceticism (vocational asceticism) can accept only the rationally regulated marriage" (Weber in Gerth and C. Wright Mills 1958:349).

Marianne Weber, wife of Max Weber, indicates a positive function of marriage because it "elevates the woman as "wife" to a position above concubines" ([1912] 2003:86). She defends the marital ideal when she writes:

Modern women value marriage as it should be – that is, a life partnership that is founded on the affinity of souls and senses, and on the desire for full responsibility, as the highest ideal of human community that stands as an unshakable guiding star above the sexual life of civilized humanity (p. 94).

Marianne Weber critiques male authority, and pleads for more egalitarian marriages and autonomy on the part of the wife by way of legal reforms because she wanted to liberate women from their historically subordinate position.

Contemporary Views: Twentieth Century Theories
Structural-functionalists

Structural- functionalists focus on the functions of the family. Traditionally, the family has served several functions: regulating sexual behavior; procreation and child rearing; education; socialization; and care for the sick and elderly. Currently, the family serves the following manifest functions: reproduction, socialization and economic activities. The family is "a mediator of social values" and serves as "an agent of social placement for the new members of society, and by acting as an agent of control for marital relations, it regulates social alliances between family units and helps to place individuals into a patterned network of interweaving social relationships" (Rose Laub Coser 2004:14).

Elman and London (2001) cluster functions of (re)marriage at the beginning of the 20th century along three dimensions: an economic function, a welfare function and a kinship function. The economic function centers on resources (gather and distribute) for the family's standard of living. The welfare function refers to providing housing and other types of assistance for dependents of all ages who would otherwise be provided for in institutional environments (i.e., foster care, homes for the elderly). The kinship function pertains to mutual support and companionship. The authors write: "Most turn-of-the-twentieth-century marriages followed marital dissolution resulting from widowhood. Remarriage was one strategy that individuals could undertake that would result in the formation of new dyads or larger social units." (p. 438). Women use remarriage as a strategy to obtain financial support. "Men, in contrast, tended to remarry for immediate instrumental assistance with children and household management, allowing them to continue their economic activities." (p. 410). However, Elman and London note that the kinship function (support and companionship) has become increasingly important throughout the last century.

Family functions have eroded in the past decades. Lasch (1975) views marriage as "an institution that supposedly provides a refuge from the competitive free-for-all but increasingly submits to pressures from without." (p. 61). Thus, even this function of the family (providing a refuge) is declining.

According to Sweeney (1997), remarriage still fulfills several functions: a need for love and companionship (the aforementioned kinship function) and instrumental benefits such as an increase in socio-economic status (the aforementioned economic function). Good socio-economic prospects will increase both men's and women's prospects of remarriage.

Famous sociologist Talcott Parsons (1943) notes that the American family is best characterized as an "open, multilineal conjugal system" (p. 24). In his view, the ego, through marriage, is a member of two conjugal families, who becomes separated from the family of orientation – both from parents and from siblings. Parsons describes a weakened relationship with kin as a result of marriage:

> But with us this transition is accompanied by a process of "emancipation" from the ties both to parents and to siblings, which is considerably more drastic than in most kinship systems, especially in that it applies to both sexes about equally, and includes emancipation from solidarity with *all* members of the family of orientation about equally, so that there is relative little continuity with *any* kinship ties established by birth for anyone (p. 32, italics by Parsons).

Parsons further states, "the importance of the isolated conjugal family unit is brought out by the fact that it is the normal "household" unit" (p. 27). In Parsons (1943) view, the structure of the American family resembles the structure of an onion in that there are several layers. In adulthood the family of procreation becomes the inner layer and parents and siblings are relocated to the second tier. Extended family members are part of the outer layers. Indeed, in their research, Hoyt and Babchuck (1983) found a closeness in the inner layer of Parsons' onion since their research shows that adults prefer members of their family of procreation as their confidante, in particular their spouse.

Social Exchange and Social Comparison Theories

Blumstein and Kollock (1988) critique structural functionalism for their over-socialized image of close relationships and argue for the need to treat family relationships as interpersonal close relationships. They conclude that interdependence is "the central defining characteristic of relationships" (p. 476), and critique sociological approaches when they state: "It is unfortunate that more sociologists have not yet turned their attention to the study of interpersonal relationships, for those hold the promise of uncovering the fabled missing link between micro and macro social processes" (p. 486).

Exchange theories, in particular social exchange theories, assume that human beings are social beings. Humans live together and work together. They do not exist in a vacuum but interact with each other. Social life must be innately rewarding given the fact that "men used to hunt in packs" (Homans 1974:27). Humans need each other. They exchange resources such as goods, services, information, money, status, and love. One can engage in social interaction and exchange for several goals. Those purposes range the gamut from instrumental (e.g., work together with people in organizations in exchange for a salary) to affectual/emotional (e.g., socialize with friends for fun).

Humans are mutually interdependent. However, whenever two or more people interact there are costs and benefits (rewards) involved. In general, people strive to have a balance between their costs and their benefits in a variety of contexts such as in an intimate relationship, in kinship associations and in work settings (see for an overview Meertens and von Grumbkow 1988).

Social comparison theory (Festinger 1954) states that people compare themselves with others and evaluate their relative position in comparison to others. They compare their beliefs to others' beliefs and they compare their input (costs) to their output (rewards). They further compare the input and output of the other person to their own. Social comparison is especially important and salient in uncertain and stressful situations. It is a human given that people compare themselves to others. Children (as young as 30 months) engage in social comparison processes (Koch 1960). They are sensitive to differential parental behavior and monitor the interaction between parent(s) and sibling(s). They are especially keen on evaluating the distribution of parental affection and attention to the self as compared to their sibling(s) (e.g., Dunn and Plomin 1991; Dunn and McGuire 1994).

Adams (1965) states that people in general desire equity in their lives and in their relationships with others. It is not the perception of equity or the seeking of equity, but rather avoiding inequity, which motivates people's behavior. In other words, people tend to be aware of situations that are inequitable and they attempt to restore equity. 'Getting even' in a situation of perceived inequity is a strategy for restoring balance.

Other exchange theories (e.g., Buss 1999; Daly, Wilson and Weghorst 1982; Euler and Weitzel 1996) focus on exchange relationships in terms of mate selection (e.g., she has the good genes, he has the material resources), and inclusive fitness (e.g., investment tendencies in siblings' offspring as a strategy for enhancing one's own inclusive fitness).

George Homans, a social behaviorist, focused on defining general laws pertaining to human behavior, both on the individual and the group level. Influenced by Skinner, a behaviorist, Homans tried to identify principles of organismic behavior (e.g., pigeons, rats or humans). He focuses on the individual and on small groups because man learns social behavior in small groups and because small groups are elements of larger social units. Homans saw no use for structural explanations of human behavior. "Structural explanation is really no explanation at all. Functional explanation leads to false consciousness as well as true ones, and it is intellectually unsatisfying at best. There remains the psychological types of explanation" (1969:209). Thus, Homans reduces human behavior to the individual level.

According to Homans, the norms of society arise from the mutual relations of individuals; we therefore need to analyze individuals and their behavior. Homans views the social system as: "the activities, interactions, and sentiments of the group members together with the mutual relations of these elements with one another during the time the group is active..." (Homans 1950:87). Homans is not interested in attitudes, instead, he focuses on activities and activities refer to "things people do" (Homans [1961] 1974:34). In other words: activities that can be observed.

Exchange sociologist Blau made a distinction between social exchange and economic exchange. In his view, social exchange is about establishing and cementing friendship bonds and entails "unspecified obligations" (1964:93), whereas economic exchange is defined strictly in the monetary sense. Expanding on social exchange, Blau terms it "...voluntary actions of individuals that are motivated by the returns they are expected to bring and typically do in fact bring from others" (1964:91). What Blau contributes are elements of social comparison theory and equity theory.

In social exchange people take note of obligation, trust, and gratitude. We trust someone to return the favor and when we deem that person not trustworthy, we discontinue providing favors. In a strict economic exchange the balance is more straightforward: when we lend someone $20, we want $20 back and do not settle for $5. The situation can get more complicated when an employee feels that he is not getting paid enough for his work. He can justify not giving notice because of lack of alternatives, he can justify staying on the job by giving less effort (e.g., doing the absolute minimum which with he can get away with), or he can justify it by perceiving that the other potential incentives, such as a high status, compensate the current pay. As Blau notes "some social rewards cannot be bartered in exchange, notably intrinsic attraction to a person, approval of his opinions and judgment, respect for his abilities, because their significance rests on their being spontaneous reactions rather than calculated means of pleasing him." (1964:99).

What Homans neglects to specify when discussing his propositions, Blau addresses. Blau stresses the importance of context in social exchange. "The social context in which exchange transactions take place affects them profoundly..." (1964:104). For instance, the 'role-set' and status of each partner in a dyad, such as in an intimate relationship, affects their exchange relationship in terms of costs and benefits pertaining to their association (e.g., foregoing other lovers). Further, coalitions between weaker members of a group can prevent a stronger group member from fully exploiting his or her possibilities. Finally, Blau addresses the potential existence of several exchange relations in the same setting, which may not be obvious but nevertheless salient. For example, an employee who works hard may garner rewards from an employer, but elicit disapproval from his co-workers who do not like the fact that he is raising the bar and, as a consequence, he may be treated as a pariah. The same concept applies to families and the alliances and exchanges that take place within the family, whether it is a traditional nuclear family or a remarried family.

Rational choice theory, as an economic exchange theory, centers on actors as maximizers of their utility. The theory is based on neo-classical economic assumptions of decision-making. It is expected that the individual or actor wants to maximize rewards and minimize costs, so that one profits overall. When actors make decisions they do so on the basis of an optimal choice after identifying the problem, collecting and sorting the information, comparing viable alternative solutions and sorting alternatives along preferences. Rational choice theory includes experiments pertaining to decision-making processes, such as the decision to compete or to cooperate in the prisoner dilemma game (Miller, Hickson, and Wilson 1996).

According to Fan and Lui, rational choice provides explanations pertaining to stay/leave decisions in marriage when women are confronted with a cheating husband. "Then in a framework of rational choice, an individual will choose to divorce if and only if one's expected utility from one's future alternatives after divorce is greater than one's utility from remaining married. An individual's future alternatives include one's perspective of remarriage" (2004:443). Factors included in this utilitarian choice model are: quality of the marital relationship before the discovery of the extramarital affair; length of marriage; wife's age; number of dependent children; wife's income; husband's income; and religious beliefs. When these factors are plugged into the equation, a stay/leave decision supposedly can be predicted. Although elegant in its methodology, "the authors assume individuals are rational and forward looking in their responses to their spouses' involvement in extramarital affairs" (Fan and Lui 2004:450). However, do human beings make decisions based on rationality alone and keep emotions out of this equation? The concept of marital satisfaction itself is a psychological concept that enters into this rational choice model. Length of marriage is also an indicator of investments made in the marital relationship and thus ties into social comparison theory and equity theory.

Economist Parkman (2004) notes that the emphasis in spousal relationships has shifted from material well being to psychological well being. In particular, when a woman's need for empathy, understanding, and acknowledgements of her contributions, are not met she is likely to seek a divorce. In layman's terms: she is not getting what she wants and therefore leaves.

Friedman and Hechter (1990) assert that individuals join groups in order to receive collective goods. The free–rider problem (the person who does not contribute equally but nevertheless receives collective goods) can be eliminated only through control mechanisms (not normative consensus). However, the key is to know the preference schedules of the actors since their preferences shape their behavior. Do people really possess full information when decisions are made? Rational choice theories remain a post facto (after the facts) explanation. Friedman and Hechter (1990) acknowledge this type of critique and the shortcomings of rational choice theories when they mention that so far a theory about preference formation has not been developed. Blau (1997) also acknowledges limitations of rational choice theories.

Exchange theories and rational choice theories have in common that they assume people are rational and motivated to get what they want. Social psychological exchange theories take values into account as well as subjective perceptions of equity.

Both rational choice theories and socio-biological theories have in common that they overemphasize the self-interest, egoistical, and utilitarian tendencies of humans. However, not everything in life, not every aspect of human interaction revolves around a cost-benefit analysis. These theories seem to reduce human nature to stock market principles of investments and returns. Further, the notion of self-interest, as articulated by Friedman and Hechter, seems to invoke competition and revolves around so-called free riders, who benefit from the collective goods but invest nothing. The authors are not explicit about the fact that there are situations when the option of cooperation is in people's best interest, such as in the case of remarried families where new family members have to cooperate in order to make the remarriage successful.

Evolutionary Theories and Views about Sexuality

Sociobiologist Wilson focuses on the biological roots of marriage and the family. He notes, "the flattened sexual cycle and continuous female attractiveness cement the close marriage bonds that are basic to human social life" (1975:548). Accordingly, the practice of reciprocal altruism within a marriage is assumed. Wilson perceives the nuclear family as a cornerstone of human society in which there exists a basic division of labor: the male provides, and the female nurses and engages in household chores.

Evolutionary psychologists address the degree of parental investment according to inclusive fitness theories (e.g., Davis and Daly 1997; Keller 2000), and the potential hostile and abusive environment in remarried families, in particular infanticide and sexual abuse of children by their non-biologically related step-parent (Daly and Wilson 1998). In addition, the degree of sibling solidarity is assumed to reflect the degree of relatedness (e.g., Hamilton 1964). From this viewpoint, siblings' relationships with full siblings are stronger than siblings' relationships with half siblings and stepsiblings. Along evolutionary lines, investment tendencies and emotional closeness between intergenerational dyads is explained with mother-daughter relationships ranking at the top and mother-in-law/daughter-in-law somewhere at the bottom. Given divorce and custody arrangements, investment in a daughter's offspring is less of a risk than investment in a son's offspring (Euler, Hoier and Rohde 2001). These scholars also argue that affinal kin (kin acquired through marriage) evoke less feelings of obligation than consanguinal (genetically related) kin.

Are individuals in families primarily interested in self-serving utilitarian strategies with or without allies within the family or are they focused on cooperation within the family and displaying appropriate amounts of solidarity in order to enhance the cohesion within the entire family? After a divorce, children who bond with their remaining family unit (e.g., mother and siblings) may not perceive their mother's remarriage as an ideal situation for them, and eventually create an us-versus-them (the stepfamily members) atmosphere in which everyone will lose since the remarriage would not be a success and the biological mother or father will be placed in the middle of this battle.

Expanding on Weber, postmodernist Michel Foucault describes how sex, through Christian values, became confined to the home because marriage became the only legitimate basis for sexual relationships. Sex is "centered on matrimonial relationships" (1978:37) and the appropriate locus is the matrimonial bedroom. Seventeenth century Europe was more open about sex, and in other societies, such as India and China, the depiction of sexual pleasure in works of art was common. However, since the Victorian Bourgeoisie and the emphasis on Christian values (e.g., the flesh as cause of all evil), our society continues to repress sex and sexuality. According to Foucault, the regulation of sex is a useful tool because it ensures population replacement and growth as well as the reproduction of labor capital. Christian values penetrate sex education in contemporary American schools. Teachings are primarily focused on abstinence until marriage. The message to American children is not to engage in any sexual activity until it is legitimized within the institution of marriage.

The next section examines feminist perspectives on the family. With a few exceptions, these perspectives all stem from a critical stance and are theoretically rooted in conflict theory, providing a Marxist and a neo-Marxist viewpoint.

Feminist Perspectives

Feminist scholars focus on marriage and the family from a perspective of oppression of women and children, rooted in the patriarchal family and twentieth century society. This section reviews the feminist movement, its stance on the sex-based division of labor within the family and its outcomes.

After the first feminist wave in the early 1920s, the feminist movement in the United States remained dormant until the early 1960s, although some women engaged in political activism or praxis. For example, Ella Bloor, a white middle class divorced mother of six children became the icon or 'Mother' of the American Communist Party. Her political activism was based on the premise that family (home) and community are the locations for class-consciousness, class struggle, and ultimately the communist revolution. She compared women's oppression and inequalities to the oppression of the working masses, as she herself was forced to generate an income and thus had to work outside the home (Brown 1999). Bloor expanded the critique on capitalist development with issues of everyday life in the community and household struggle. Specifically, Ella Bloor was interested in making this world a better world for women and children by targeting issues such as child labor, poverty, exploitation of women in all industries, and unemployment.

Unlike Comte and Simmel, Bloor did not want to separate the private and the public spheres because she was convinced that these spheres are intertwined. Mothers were seen as united across class, race, and nation. She fought for emancipation of women and for the underprivileged working class and rejected male domination in the communist party in favor of integration of women, children, and community.

Some of her ideas clashed with the prevalent beliefs of the communist party in the 1920s that the party should focus solely on exploited workers in non-unionized heavy industry, thus excluding members of the proletariat who did not engage in wage labor, such as housewives and young children. The general assumption in the communist party was that oppression of women would be resolved after the revolution and abolishment of private property as the source of all evil.

Critics of Bloor focus on what they see as her inability to understand Marxist theory. It is not the family and the neighborhood (community) that is the loci of class struggle but the working conditions of the masses. Other critics argue that Ella Bloor through the label 'Mother' was de-politicized and de-sexed. In other words, 'Mother' implies that she is not a sexually active female and need not to be taken serious in her political rhetoric (see for an overview Brown 1999). Further, Bloor is accused of maternalism, which emphasizes the woman's role of mother and applies the characteristics of that role - mothering, caretaking, nurturance, and morality - to society as a whole. Maternalism assumes that all women have natural mothering capacities, such as an innate capacity to nurture, and therefore men and women occupy separate spheres. Men dominate the public sphere, whereas women dominate the private sphere. We have seen earlier that classical sociologists such as Comte view this division of labor as natural.

According to Betty Friedan, American suburban housewives struggled tremendously in the 1950s and 1960s because they were confined to their homes doing domestic labor and care-taking chores, while at the same time they had to "glorify in their own femininity" ([1963] 1999:356). They were supposed to find a husband and bear children. By the end of the 1950s more young women enjoyed the benefits of higher education, but nevertheless dropped out of college to marry. Soon a new degree was named for wives of college students: "Ph.T. (Putting Husbands Through)" ([1963] 1999:357).

The difference between couples who married in the 1950s and couples who married in the 1970s is clearly a shift from a traditional model of marriage to a more egalitarian relationship between the marital partners. Hackstaff makes a distinction between 'marriage talk' and 'divorce talk' in a divorce-ridden society. She notes, "A wife or husband is empowered if their spouse believes in "marriage as forever" because they can count on the spouse to ride out turbulent transitions" (1999:100). She further notes that marriages are still centered on men's terms and observes: "A full-blown marital work ethic has arisen because of divorce anxiety and marital instability, yet it has also risen because of instabilities in beliefs about gender. Spouses must be reflexive about the nature of marriage culture since the authority of marriage culture and male dominance have lost their hegemonic hold" (1999:294).

There exists an ongoing debate between Marxist feminists whether domestic labor is alienating housewives (Donovan 1985). One may argue that domestic labor is alienating. Women have no freedom of choice; once married they are confined to the house and thus to domestic labor. However, women have freedom in choosing their domestic chores, they have degrees of freedom (i.e., in when they are doing which chore) and task variety. Further, housewives produce products (i.e., cooking meals), and in that sense their labor can be considered use value labor and thus domestic labor may be regarded as intrinsically rewarding and not alienating.

In contemporary society, a growing number of married women with children participate in the labor force. The labor force participation rate for mothers with children younger than 18 years was 70 percent in 2004 (United States Department of Labor 2005). In addition, Schor (1991) notes a rising workload in the United States, which leads to stress, sleep deficits, child neglect, and the concept of juggling work and family needs. In short, the trend is that fathers are working longer hours, mothers increasingly work and they also work longer hours. This translates in less time for family compared to decades ago when fewer married women worked outside the home and fathers were spending less time at work. The family is in a 'time crunch', while at the same time experiencing more challenges given structural changes in family life such as divorce and remarriage.

Women are not organized in a certain class. Rather, they are still defined in terms of to whom they are married or to whom they belong. It is therefore difficult to mobilize women in revolution, as women experience life differently. The woman married to an upper class man who has her own housekeeper, nanny, and cook, and the time and money to engage in creative labor, such as the arts, will probably not perceive her situation as alienating.

Whether or not a woman derives pride from her domestic labor, her position is always defined in terms of her family or, as Simone de Beauvoir states it in 1949, as Other. "Thus humanity is male and man defines woman not in herself but as relative to him; she is not regarded as an autonomous being" ([1949] 1999:337). She further adds: "Man can think of himself without woman. She cannot think of herself without man" ([1949] 1999:337). Thus, women are defined in terms of their social relationships or kinship relationships. They are defined in terms of the male to whom they are connected. Women are classified early in life as daughter of and sister of. Later in life when they have found a husband, women are defined as wife of and mother of. "The couple is a fundamental unity with its two halves riveted together, and the cleavage of society along the line of sex is impossible. Here is to be found the basic trait of woman: she is the Other in a totality of which the two components are necessary to one another" ([1949] 1999:339). These remnants of patriarchy are still present in our contemporary American society. Consider for example the Church or Temple, which addresses – in the year 2004 – correspondence to Mr. and Mrs. John Smith. She apparently has no first name of her own but is referred to as her husband's appendix.

Iulina and Scanlan (1996) state that it does not really matter what a housewife's household duties pertain to since a housewife's main purposes are reproduction and socialization of labor power, and creating conditions for restoring the energies of the workers. Therefore she creates, revives, and reproduces capital. For these reasons, through her husband, a housewife is also an object of exploitation. In this manner, Iulina and Scanlan basically make the same case as Ella Bloor: the family is the locus of class struggle and class-consciousness.

For radical feminist Andrea Dworkin (1981) it is not class struggle but domination of men over women that is the real problem. This domination takes place not only in the home, and thus in the family, but in our capitalist society and market system in the form of pornography. Through pornography, men possess women as men derive different kinds of power over women reflected in power of money and notably in power of sex.

Heidi Hartmann views the patriarchal system as the source of inequalities between men and women. She argues that before capitalism was introduced, men already controlled the labor of women and children in the domain of the family. "The roots of women's present social status lie in this sex ordered division of labor" ([1976] 1992:99). In her view, the hierarchical nature of the division of labor between the sexes must be eliminated, as well as the division of labor itself.

The social constructionist approach views gender as a social construct that embodies cultural meanings of masculinity and femininity. Gender is an element of social structures and interwoven with other social structures such as class and race. Values and privileges are assigned on the basis of sex. Traditionally, men have been systematically privileged over women. Men and women have to be constantly reminded, by society on a macro level, and in the family and work setting on an individual level, to be masculine or feminine.

Feminism assumes that women and men are of equal importance in social action. Feminist inquiry is unified by the belief that females and males, femininity and masculinity are equally valuable. Feminist scholars seek to identify critique and alter structures and practices that actively or passively hinder equality. "The axis of feminist inquiry is gender, which consists of deeply ensconced social meanings and their derivative power. Not a codeword for women, gender is a cultural construction that profoundly affects women, men, and relationships between them" (Fox and Murray 2000:1160).

All feminists, including Marxist feminists, Freudian feminists (e.g., Chodorow [1978] 1999), radical lesbian feminists, and Black feminists are united in their perspective on feminine scholarship (e.g., Allen 2000; Fox and Murray 2000). These authors expand on earlier critiques of Dorothy Smith on the sociological method of inquiry which is examined in chapter four.

Postmodern society has high expectations for women and thus puts pressure on them. They have come of age in a time when it is expected that "a successful woman combines marriage to a communicative, egalitarian man with motherhood and an engaging rewarding career" (Stacey [1996] 1999:650). Whereas the modern woman needed to adhere to the norm of female homemaker, the postmodern woman needs to adhere to a different norm. The postmodern view also puts masculinity in a different perspective: "As working-class men's access to breadwinner status has receded, so too has their confidence in their masculinity (Stacey [1996] 1999:651). As a result, not everyone hails the accomplishments of the women's movement and feminist scholars.

Betty Friedan was content with the accomplishments of the women's movement. In a 1998 interview, she points out that the women's movement has booked tremendous success during the last decades of the twentieth century. In particular, she states that women have become a potent force in politics, the gender-wage gap is diminishing, more women earn college degrees and motherhood has become a choice. Friedan sees it as a mission for the women's movement to focus on a life in which family and work are balanced for both sexes. "So far family needs and family issues have been defined as the woman's domain. The next frontier is to make it the man's as well. Children ought to be seen as the equal responsibility of men and women". She further notes, "As women are now entitled to equal opportunity in the workplace, men should be considered equally responsible for the family" (Friedan in Gardels 1998:59-60). Friedan's message is clear: the women's movement has been successful in eradicating some of the inequalities between the sexes. Despite men's increasing contributions to the 'typically female domain', women still perform the majority of household chores and childcare related activities (e.g., Bahr and Ahlander 1995; Hochschild 1997; Riley and Kiger 1999; Sanchez 1996).

Throughout the last half of the twentieth century, marriage in general developed from traditional (i.e., based on male authority) to more egalitarian, where both spouses share the power in their relationship and in which husbands accommodate their wives' work. During her research regarding married couples, Hackstaff observed, "the transition to equality can strain a relationship and threaten to unravel a marriage" (1999:88). Gottman and his colleagues Coan, Carrere and Swanson (1998) note that men, who accept influence from their wives and thus give room to an egalitarian marriage relationship, tend to have happy and stable marriages. Apparently there is some truth in the proverbial 'A happy wife is a happy life'.

Byfield (1999) argues that the institution of the nuclear family has collapsed since the sexual revolution in the 1960s. Birth control became readily available, abortion became legal, and due to no-fault divorce laws, divorce was easier to obtain. As a result, sex was no longer attached to procreation, procreation became detached from parenting and parenting was detached from marriage. Accordingly, in Byfield's view, because the family was no longer necessary, appropriate gender roles became obsolete. "Without the family gender is irrelevant" (1999:4). Byfield further adds, "Our attempts to ignore sex differences have created vast seas of loneliness, frustration, and violence by both sexes, not just men. But sex differences exist for a natural reason, and if we ignore it, nothing we do will work" (1999:4). The point that emerges from Byfield's argument is a protection of traditional family values to avoid gender confusion and its negative consequences. Therefore, he is on 'the same page' as proponents for family values such as scholars affiliated with the Institute for American Values.

Currently, as we have seen, the majority of women work in the paid labor force. Women now do have a choice in deciding whether they want to pursue a career. Therefore, they are prone to the same exploitation that was imposed on men. Although decreased, the gender wage gap still exists. Women with the same level of education and expertise as men are still paid less for the same job performance. Women now have two jobs: paid labor and household and care-taking duties. "Women are the ones who shoulder most of the workload at home" (Hochschild [1997] 1999:656). The economic pressures on the family are real. Parents need tax relief and work relief in order to take care of their children (Gallagher 1997). This need is in direct opposition to workplace demands.

Carnoy (1999) discusses that work in our postmodern society requires stable and well-organized families of which each adult member is able to operate in a flexible work environment. This postmodern work environment, however, is characterized by job instability, which causes family members to change their work situations often. Further, new jobs may require the acquisition of new skills, thus more education, and may require relocation thereby disrupting the family unit. The author notes: "in a flexible work system the family is at the hub of productive and reproductive activity" (p. 420). Carnoy observes that work situations in postmodern society require adaptable and flexible stable families, thereby ignoring the ongoing interaction between the two institutions of work and family.

Summary

The existing body of research explains marriage and family formation in terms of inheritance, economic needs, sexual needs, and social needs. The institution of marriage is the only government approved legal umbrella for sexual relationships, cohabitation, and procreation. Marriage still serves important functions, namely socialization of new members and providing companionship. Within marriages, there still exists a gender-based division of labor that is perceived by some as exploitative of wives. Marriage, divorce, and remarriage decisions are rational, emotional, and psychological in nature and involve numerous factors.

The overwhelming academic focus is on traditional middle class nuclear families and whenever remarriage is studied, stepparent-child relationships, and spousal relationships in the binuclear family are the main foci. Other family constellations have been understudied. Contemporary research has at best generated middle range theories in explaining family processes.

In our contemporary postmodern U.S. society, family and work put pressure on the individuals involved. Given women's increasing labor force participation, marriage for economic reasons is less a necessity, as is marriage for purposes of establishing proof of paternity because current technology can establish paternity by using DNA samples. Although some scholars argue that marriage is on the decline as an institution since the divorce rate is so high, I would argue that this is not the case. Marriage continues to be seen as a valuable institution as so many people decide to marry, and moreover, are motivated to marry again after a divorce. For many, marriage is seen as valuable since it provides an optimal environment for child rearing. Given these facts, we can expect more traditional nuclear families to become bi-nuclear families or even tri-nuclear families over time. Because children are perceived as key factors in their parents' successful remarriages, we have to address sibling relationships in contemporary remarried families.

CHAPTER THREE
Sibling Relationships

This chapter explores the existing body of research pertaining to sibling relationships, sibling differentiation, sibling solidarity, and sibling rivalry. The influence of parental investment and differential parental treatment are examined, as well as the influence of the quality of the marital relationship on offspring. The existing literature pertaining to siblings in traditional nuclear or 'intact' families, where the focus is solely on full siblings, is examined for two reasons. First, we need to better understand under which conditions family dynamics shape and change sibling relationships. Second, remarried families originally started as an intact or nuclear family. Most siblings now in blended sibling groups grew up for a number of years in a traditional nuclear family constellation. Further, this chapter examines sibling relationships during and after divorce and addresses studies on sibling relationships in remarried families.

Research regarding sibling relationships has focused on siblings in traditional nuclear families (e.g., Dorfman and Mertens 1990; Miner and Uhlenberg 1997). There are few studies regarding sibling relationships in remarried or blended families (e.g., White 1994, 1998; White and Riedmann 1992a; White and Riedmann 1992b). One of the preliminary conclusions is that this type of family is potentially hazardous for children due to risks of violence, sexual abuse, and even infanticide by their non-related live-in stepparent, usually the stepfather (Daly and Wilson 1998). Further, the literature suggests that family bonds in remarried families are weaker than family bonds in traditional nuclear families, and that those bonds in remarried families are influenced by the degree of genetic relatedness (e.g., Filinson 1986; White 1998).

Another preliminary conclusion is that boys seem to fare better when their mother remarries, if certain conditions are met, such as an emotionally warm stepfather who sets limits. The existing body of research pertaining to the blended family, as well as representations of stepfamilies in the media, have reinforced the negative portrayal of this type of family and even stigmatized it (Jones 2003; Leon and Angst 2005). Children in homes with stepparents are rated as having more behavioral problems and a tendency to delinquent behavior (e.g., Skeen et al. 1984). Indeed, Hetherington, one of the most prominent family scholars, notes that compared to children in traditional nuclear families, children in divorced and remarried families display more problems (10 percent versus 20 to 25 percent respectively). As to the risk of teen pregnancy, she remarks that girls in divorced and "especially remarried families attain puberty much earlier and are more likely to become involved with older male peers" (2003:233). However, in her conclusion she sends the upbeat message that "the vast majority are resilient and able to cope with, or even benefit from their new life situation" (2003:234).

Sibling Differentiation

Why children within the same family are as different from each other as they are has been a puzzle to researchers in the social sciences. Apparently, personality differences between siblings are so significant that sibling differentiation has been much more often studied than have processes that tend toward solidarity between siblings who are born in the same family. Differences between children have been the subject of studies mainly in the psycho-pathological tradition with an emphasis on psychology and behavior genetics. Identical twins separated at an early age and reared in different families turned out to be more similar than identical twins separated at a much later time. Even though they are reared together, growing up in the same family appears to make siblings different rather than similar (Deal, Halverson and Wampler 1994; Lalumière, Quinsey and Craig

1996; Reiss, Plomin, Hetherington, Howe, Rovine, Tyron and Hagan 1994; Sulloway 1996).

In their review article discussing prior research in this area, Dunn and Plomin (1991) conclude that thus far there is general consensus that siblings are very different from each other and that heredity accounts for only a small portion of the resemblance between full siblings. Although full siblings share roughly 50 percent of their genes, they only correlate about 0.15 in personality traits. They are, thus, as the authors conclude, as different from each other as anyone chosen at random from a large population. As genetics do not account for the majority of differences between full siblings, Dunn and Plomin state that the source of sibling differences may be attributed to the shared family environment.

Psychologists traditionally have sought to explain and attribute sibling differences to the non-shared environment (e.g., peers and teachers) and they have assumed that the family creates the same environment for each sibling within that family. The marital relationship and the emotional family climate are shared parts of the family environment; however, siblings may experience those shared parts of the family environment differently. Apparently, it is within the family environment that differentiation among siblings is elicited or triggered (Daniels 1986).

Most of the studies that pertain to siblings have addressed parent-child interactions with a theoretical emphasis on attachment theory and a strong focus on mother-child interactions, as the mother is usually the child's primary caregiver. Early attachment of the child to the mother is seen as essential to the maintenance of close relationships in later life. Because of this perspective, associations among the father-child relationship and the sibling-sibling relationship have been understudied.

Attachment is important for the perception of cohesive families. Research indicates that young adults with secure attachment styles view their families as more emotionally close, adaptable, and satisfying than young men and women with insecure avoidant or insecure anxious-ambivalent attachment styles (Pfaller, Kiselica, and Gerstein 1998). From an attachment theory perspective, the presence of both parents forms an early basis for developing a sense of trust in their offspring. In a longitudinal study, King (2002) found a pervasive negative effect of divorce on children trusting their fathers. They are more likely to distrust their father after a divorce; however, this phenomenon does not impact their trust in a romantic partner later in life.

A second important mainstream theoretical perspective on sibling issues derives from family systems theory. This approach emphasizes that every family member is a part of an interactive network characterized by dependency relations. The behavior of each individual member or subsystem of individuals influences the behavior of the other family member(s). Therefore, Hetherington (1994) argues that sibling relationships should not be viewed as isolated entities and she emphasizes a focus on other processes within the family. Matthews (2002) also suggests to viewing families as networks of relationships. Thus, family systems theory establishes links, not only within the parent-child relationship, but also includes the marital relationship, the extended family, non-custodial parents, and stepkin (Dunn 1988; Hetherington 1994). Kerig notes, "while family members' perceptions of the family system may differ, individuals' subjective experiences predict the impact of family relationships on them" (1995: 38).

In the next section, the discussion turns to factors that are responsible for eliciting differentiation between siblings such as birth order and parental expectations, as well as factors that promote solidarity between siblings, such as similarity in age and gender.

Family Constellation and Parental Factors

Sulloway (1996) argues that the child's place in the birth order plays a key role in the development of personality characteristics and thus differentiation among children. Siblings occupy different niches within the family. Eldest or firstborn children tend to identify more closely with parents and authority, establish parent-pleasing behavior, and have a proclivity to behave as surrogate parents toward their younger siblings. Further, firstborns tend to be ambitious, conscientious, and conforming. The second-born child is likely to be cooperative and often strives to catch up with the older sibling. Middle-born children are said to have a special talent for compromise; they are considered the diplomats of the family. The last-born child is supposed to have a propensity toward rebellion, is generally more open-minded, and is generally more open to new experiences. For example, the last-born child tends to be the most adventurous child in the family.

Birth order also has its impact on familial sentiments. Both firstborn and last-born children feel much closer to their parents and turn to their parents for emotional and financial support on a more frequent basis than middle-born children. A plausible explanation for this phenomenon is that first-born and last-born children are often the beneficiaries of parental investment. Firstborn children have a higher reproductive value as compared to their siblings primarily because they are older and, thus, parents have invested more in this child than in their younger children. Last-born children receive the undiluted attention of parents because there are no other children to be taken care of and it is usually clear to the parents that this child is their last child (Salmon and Daly 1998).

Parents respond differently to each of their children, birth order being one of the factors (Musun-Miller 1993). Parents have a different set of attributions, expectations and stereotypes for each of their children based upon their children's order of birth. Parents have more positive ratings and higher expectations of their firstborn child. They perceive their eldest child as less spoiled and more self-critical compared to their other children (Musun-Miller 1993). Parents have high expectations of their oldest child, especially about being responsible and sharing (Greer and Myers 1992). Despite the strong social norm to 'treat all your children the same', parents tend to treat their children differently based upon beliefs and expectations they have about their children (Handel 1986). For example, only a minority of mothers report "similar intensity or affection for their children or say that they give similar attention, control and discipline to their children" (Dunn and Plomin 1991:275). Differential parenting partly explains differences among siblings pertaining to antisocial behavior and depression (Feinberg and Hetherington 2001). Further, receiving less parental warmth as compared to one's sibling leads to an increase of depressive symptoms in girls, but not in boys (Shanahan, McHale, Crouter, and Osgood 2008).

The gender of the child can elicit parental differential treatment as well. Sex biased parental treatment is not uncommon. For example, among camel herding nomadic pastoralists in Kenya, favoring one child over the other is reflected in the number of animals passed on to a child at marriage. Firstborn sons are usually favored over the other children (Mace 1996). In addition, parents tend to treat their sons and daughters differently based upon their expectations and beliefs about appropriate gender behavior. One common assumption is that boys are more aggressive and girls more gentle and cooperative. These stereotypes of appropriate gender behavior should be seen in the context of culture. As outlined by cross-cultural psychologist Hofstede (1991), every culture has its own assumptions about appropriate behavior for males and appropriate behavior for females. Hofstede makes a dichotomy between masculine and feminine cultures. America is clearly a more masculine society in which boys do not cry and boys fight back when attacked. Girls, on the other hand, are allowed to cry but are not allowed to fight. In a more feminine society, such as The Netherlands, both boys and girls are allowed to cry but they may not fight. These culture-specific stereotypes are not only pervasive in childrearing practices but also affect family life, school, and work (Hofstede 1991).

The so-called 'dilution hypothesis' predicts parental investment given limited parental resources. According to this hypothesis, parents who have many children invest less time, money, emotional energy, and attention in each child. The larger the number of siblings, the less parental investment each individual child receives

(Shavitt and Pierce 1991). However, the reverse also seems the case, since the more children parents' have, the less attention and assistance a parent receives from every individual adult child in old age (Spitze and Logan 1991). These authors found that when the number of siblings increases there is less instrumental assistance from each individual child. They note that both the offspring and the parents may adjust their expectations regarding help in relation to the structure of the sibling group. The size of the sibling group also affects the status orientation of younger children because status ambitions of youngest children decrease with sibship size (Davis 1997). However, the size of the sibling group does not affect the firstborn child's status ambitions.

There appears to be a strong underlying evolutionary psychological mechanism affecting paternal investment and differential paternal treatment. Given the reproductive biology of the human species, a mother is always certain that a child born out of her body has her genes and is really her child, while a man will never be completely certain that his partner's offspring is also his offspring leading to an uncertainty on a man's part as to the fatherhood of his children.

A high paternity probability is a necessary condition for an increase in a male's parental investment in his offspring (Kurland 1979). Promiscuity and marital instability are predictors of low paternity certainty. Due to possible sexual infidelity on the part of his mate, a man has a risk of investing in an offspring that does not carry his genes (Buunk, Angleitner, Oubaid and Buss 1996; Geary 2000). Likewise, paternal affection is suggested to be sensitive to perceived resemblance. It is generally in the interest of the mother to promote confidence of paternity in order to elicit paternal investment in the child. She is thus motivated to underscore paternal similarity by naming the child after the father or his blood relatives (Daly and Wilson 1982). A remarried mother can, for example, try to enhance her spouse's interests and investment in her child by pointing out similarities in personality between the child and the stepfather, and/or by convincing her new spouse to formally adopt the child and give him or her his last name. A stepfather may be inclined to please his new wife by investing time and money in her offspring. Evolutionary psychologists consider the latter as a special form of mate investment because the investment is aimed at the new spouse through her child(ren).

More support for this evolutionary-based association between paternity uncertainty and the degree of paternal investment stems from studies conducted by Euler and Weitzel (1996) and Gaulin, McBurney and Brakemann-Wartell (1997) on investment tendencies of second-degree relatives. Paternity (un)certainty shapes the investment strategies of grandparents and aunts and uncles. Euler and Weitzel stress the higher attentiveness ratings of maternal grandfathers in their grandchildren compared to paternal grandmothers who are less certain that their son's children carry their genes. Further, uncles and aunts from the mother's side of the family invest significantly more attention and resources in their nieces and nephews than uncles and aunts from the father's side of the family. Gaulin et al. (1997) argue that uncertainty of paternity is the most likely explanation for higher levels of investment by maternal relatives. Whether social class and economic status play a role is not determined because the authors have no background data on their subjects other than that they are all undergraduate college students reporting on actual investment by second-degree relatives. Inclusive fitness theories have also been applied to explain a rank order of bereavement. Apparently, the death of a healthy male child who had a strong resemblance to his parents was grieved far more than the death of another child (Littlefield and Rushton 1986). According to inclusive fitness theory this makes sense since the parents have invested in this child and his death signifies a loss of their parental investments and eliminates any hopes of future assistance from this child.

From an evolutionary perspective, siblings are rivals because they are competing over their parents' limited resources. They display solidarity as a way to defend kin who are genetically closely related (e.g., Buss 1999; Hrdy 1987).

Children tend to have a preference for allocating their resources with siblings and friends rather than acquaintances. Cooperative, pro-social and altruistic behavior toward siblings is in line with kin selection (Knight and Chao 1991). Benefiting family members, in this case full siblings, would be advantageous not for one's own immediate reproductive success but, because of genetic relatedness, for indirect pay-off via siblings' offspring. Cooperative forms of behavior towards friends and other non-family members can be explained as a Darwinian instance of reciprocal altruism: an expectation that favors will be reciprocated in the long run. Humans tend to closely monitor cooperative and altruistic acts and their pay-off over time (Sulloway 1998). More evidence for inclusive fitness strategies is suggested by anthropologist Napoleon Chagnon (1983) who found that marriage arrangers in Yanomamo culture tend to benefit their closer kin over their more distant kin.

The degree to which people feel obliged to help varies along genetic relatedness (Piercy 1998). Favoring kin over non-kin is known as nepotism and can be explained in terms of inclusive fitness strategies. However, closeness with kin also is culturally determined by societal laws, norms and customs, as well as physical proximity and accessibility of kin for interaction (Neyer and Lang 2003). In addition, it is also suggested that people derive happiness from assisting their loved ones (Sulloway 1998).

The aforementioned differential parental treatment, the influence of birth order, sex of the child, paternal (un)certainty, and beliefs and expectations held by the parents indicate that the shared family environment is in reality not really shared: children experience their supposedly same-family environment differently.

Children's Perspectives

Most children in the United States experience the birth of a new sibling within four years of their own birth (Baydar, Hyle and Brooks-Gunn 1997). A longitudinal study dealing with the effects of the birth of a new sibling reveals that a new baby causes considerable change in the family (Baydar, Greek and Brooks-Gunn 1997). The new sibling has a negative impact on the general self-worth of the older child, and he or she tends to regress in behavior. Further, there is a decline in positive interactions between mothers and their older children, and controlling styles of parenting become more likely. As soon as a new baby is born, the older child is confronted with a rival. He or she is no longer the only child that receives the exclusive parental attention but suddenly has to share or compete for limited parental resources.

Sigmund Freud described how an older child might perceive the birth of a new sibling. According to Freud, the birth of a new sibling has a devastating impact on the older child. "But what the child grudges the unwanted intruder and rival is not only the suckling but all the other signs of maternal care. It feels that it has been dethroned, despoiled, prejudiced in its rights; it casts a jealous hatred upon the new baby and develops a grievance against the faithless mother which often finds expression in a disagreeable change in its behavior" ([1933] 1965:587). Freud further notes, "the whole shock is repeated with the birth of each new brother or sister" ([1933] 1965:587). A firstborn himself, Freud at the age of 17 months reacted at the arrival of his younger brother with rage (Gay 1988).

Research conducted by Dunn and McGuire (1994) demonstrates that the firstborn indeed protests against the attention the mother gives to the second born. In addition, a firstborn child may feel that he or she serves as a guinea pig as the parents practice their parenting on them. The oldest child may feel he or she had to battle for turf and privileges as opposed to later-born children: "The younger siblings invaded the territory the firstborn has staked out" (Greer and Myers 1992:250). Sisters and brothers vie not only for their parents' attention and physical care but also for their love, approval and intellectual stimulation (Greer and Myers 1992). The stressful transition in the family when a new child is added may be prevented when the firstborn is more than three years older than the new sibling and has already established friendships with other children through play (Kramer and Gottman 1992).

Social comparison theory states that people tend to evaluate themselves through comparison with others (Festinger 1954). Children often compare themselves with their siblings. They compare their beliefs and thus acquire knowledge of the world and ways of evaluating the self. Social comparison is especially important and salient in uncertain and stressful situations. Siblings are aware of their differences regarding personality, confidence, abilities, reactions, and feelings. They actively engage in social comparison processes in evaluating, for example, the distribution of parental attention and affection, and how their grades at school compare to other siblings. Even very young children (14 to 16 months) are sensitive to disputes, outcomes, and emotions in the family and compare themselves with each other. Thus, children at a very young age are aware of differences between themselves and their siblings. They are sensitive to differential parental behavior and monitor the interaction between parent(s) and sibling(s) (Dunn and Plomin 1991). Generally, children do not compare themselves with others until later in their development (age 7 or 8), but within the family social comparison processes start much earlier. Children can easily determine whether their mother favors them or their siblings. Children at an age of only 30 months actively engage in social comparison processes comparing the attention they get from their mother with the attention their sibling gets from the mother (Dunn and McGuire 1994).

Only since the 1980s have psychologists and sociologists systematically gathered insights into the ways children perceive their relationships with their siblings (e.g., Dunn and Kendrick 1982; Dunn and Plomin 1990; Ihinger-Tallman 1987b; Stocker, Lanthier and Furman 1997). No two siblings experience their relationship similarly. It can happen that one sibling is positive about the other while the other expresses derogatory feelings. When there are more siblings present, every member involved in the triad or larger group of siblings has his or her own opinion about the others.

In an exploratory study, Handel (1986) identified a set of issues that arise between siblings and in their relationship with their parents within the traditional nuclear family. He notes four major issues in sibling's relationships: equity, loyalty, maturity, and individuality. Equity is the most pervasive issue and is a necessary factor for a sense of solidarity between siblings. Generally, children like to be treated equally, and as mentioned before, are sensitive to the way parents treat them and their brothers and sisters. Benefiting one child over the other or assigning a scapegoat (continuously blaming one child) are perceived as inequitable situations and may, for the child who has been treated unfairly, lead to a condition of emotional disturbance.

Very closely related and interwoven with the principle of equity is the loyalty issue in sibling relationships. Every family member is expected to be loyal to his or her family. According to Handel (1986), loyalty of one sibling to another is manifested and expected along four dimensions: availability, protection, handling information properly, and sharing. Siblings desire availability of parents and siblings for support, advice, and companionship in play; the brother or sister is expected to 'be there' for his or her sibling. As we have seen in chapter two, kinship functions include emotional support and companionship (Elman and London 2001). Protection has to do with loyalty towards siblings in situations outside the family. When a younger child is involved in a physical conflict with peers, the older sibling is expected to protect the younger sibling. Information deals with the expectation that siblings should be loyal toward one another by not telling their parents on each other. Also, there is a strong expectation, when entrusted with a secret, that one keeps this secret. When these loyalty norms are violated, children attempt to 'get even'. For example, "I tell on her because she told on me". Getting even is a strategy for restoring equity. Another dimension of loyalty is sharing. Children learn the norm that the shared family membership imposes on siblings the obligation to share possessions. Children have a strong sense of equity towards sharing: "If you play with my toys, I'm allowed to play with your toys". When this expectation of sharing is not fulfilled the disappointed child is likely to become aggressive.

A third sibling issue is maturity, which is manifested as power. Older siblings often try to dominate younger siblings and this trait is manifested as knowledge. The older siblings are generally seen as having knowledge that they are obligated to share with their younger siblings. The younger child tries to learn from his or her older sibling; the older sibling often perceives this as a form of pestering (Handel 1986).

Another important issue in sibling relationships is individuality. Siblings want to set limits to loyalty claims. Ways of setting limits include privacy, which involves jurisdiction over one's own space (e.g., a room), and personal ownership of possessions (e.g., toys). This individuality issue can easily provoke conflicts regarding the loyalty issue of sharing. Insistence on privacy and personal ownership of possessions is a way of demarcating the self, within the shared family identity. Other ways of demarcating the self, or attaining individuality are through birth order (e.g., I am the oldest child) and gender (e.g., I am the boy of the family).

These sibling issues -loyalty, equity, maturity, and individuality - cause conflict between siblings. They are interwoven through expectations and norms that ought to be met. In social exchange theory terms, these expectations of siblings can be labeled as "unspecified obligations" (Blau 1964:93). These loyalty obligations are important and even crucial in establishing and cementing friendship bonds between siblings. Rivalry, hostility, and aggressiveness are basic features of sibling relationships. Sibling rivalry is in fact one of the primary features of sibling relationships (Handel 1986).

Given the emphasis on the aforementioned issue of equity in sibling relationships and its expectations, it is appropriate to invoke equity theory. Adams

(1965) states that people in general desire equity in their lives and in their relationships with others. It is not the perception of equity or the seeking of equity, but rather avoiding inequity, which motivates people's behavior. In other words, people tend to be aware of situations that are inequitable and they attempt to restore equity. 'Getting even' in a situation of perceived inequity is a strategy for restoring balance. This strategy also makes a sibling aware, that, in social exchange terms, 'unspecified obligations' are not met, and that the sibling ought to accommodate one's brother or sister.

The sibling issue of sharing toys and other possessions ties into principles of economic exchange theories. There is an expectation that the exchange of goods should be reciprocated, and children monitor those exchanges in terms of 'You played with my toy, I play with yours'. Apparently, some of Blau's 'unspecified obligations' are in reality, among siblings, clearly specified. Children keep track of exchanges and when they are deemed unsatisfactory or inequitable, children become hostile and aggressive toward their sibling. When hostility and aggressiveness do not have the desired effect (reciprocity and thereby restoring an inequitable situation), the child may give up on his or her sibling altogether, and bow out of any relationship with the sibling, thereby following rational choice theory principles. In this instance, because they still have to live in the same household, a child may decide to withhold any investments in the particular sibling and avoid that sibling as much as possible.

Quality of Sibling Relationships

Furman and Buhrmester (1985) identified four quality dimensions in sibling relationships: warmth and closeness, relative power and status, conflict, and rivalry. Their study found that children felt greater feelings of warmth and closeness toward same-sex siblings than toward opposite sex ones. Children of the same-sex who were close in age reported the strongest feelings on this dimension. Thus, similarity in age and gender between siblings promotes relationships that resemble friendships. In addition, Cicirelli's (1995) research showed that dyads consisting of sisters are much closer than all other dyad compositions (brother-brother, brother-sister). The second quality dimension, relative power and status, showed that older members of dyads were dominant over their younger siblings. This is especially true when siblings are widely spaced with an age difference of at least four years. Children who were four or more years younger than their sibling reported they had the least power or status and engaged in the least amount of nurturing or care-taking behavior. Further, there is a significant age-effect on the conflict dimension. Children reported more conflict with narrowly-spaced siblings than with widely-spaced ones. In other words, children quarreled more with siblings closer in age. Finally, rivalry is greater when siblings are younger rather than older. Feelings of rivalry with widely spaced younger siblings were particularly present in families of four or more children.

The partly contradictory findings that close in age same-sex siblings reported the greatest feelings of warmth and closeness while simultaneously reporting high levels of competition and conflict is explained by the authors. Furman and Buhrmester (1985) suggest that because of the friendship resemblance of the relationship between these siblings, conflict may be avoided in order not to threaten the continuation of this friendship. Further, the institutional structure of the family allows frequent expression of conflict because it guarantees the 'survival' of sibling relationships. Within traditional nuclear families, siblings cannot divorce their siblings; their kinship remains forever.

The authors further state that the child-parent relationship influences the sibling relationship. Not surprisingly, parental partiality was associated with feelings of competition and conflict. Parents who are responsive to their children's behavior in an equitable way tend to foster pro-social behavior such as cooperation, loyalty, and sharing. Brody, Stoneman and McCoy (1994) found similar results. In their study, three types of sibling relationships emerged: typical, harmonious and conflicted. Typical sibling relationships (44 percent of the dyads) were characterized by moderate levels of both warmth and conflict. These children reported considerable levels of intimacy, companionship, affection, and pro-social behavior. Children in typical sibling relationships also reported considerable levels of quarreling, antagonism, and competition. Children in harmonious sibling relationships (23 percent of the dyads) experienced considerable warmth and very little conflict. The third style of sibling relationships is the conflicted relationship, found in 33 percent of the dyads. These children manifested low to moderate levels of warmth and high levels of conflict. The authors also identified an association between the marital relationship of the parents, the emotional climate of the family, and the type of sibling relationship. Parents whose children have typical sibling relationships display less inter-parental conflict and a more positive emotional family climate than parents of conflicted siblings. Further, parents of harmonious siblings have a higher marital quality and a more positive emotional family climate than parents of siblings in typical and conflicted relationships.

In addition, Brody, Stoneman and McCoy (1994) demonstrated a link between differential treatment and the conflicted sibling relationship style. Mothers and fathers of siblings in the conflicted group displayed higher rates of negative behavior than did those of siblings in the typical and harmonious groups. The authors note that there are developmental changes in sibling relationships from middle childhood to early adolescence. These developmental changes are similar to Handel's (1986) concept of individuality, demarcating the self from the family identity. Some siblings detach themselves a little from their whole family and maintain harmonious relationships, whereas others compete, leading to an increase in rivalry and a decrease in companionship levels.

The three sibling relationship styles (harmonious, typical, and conflicted) which emerged in Brody, Stoneman and McCoy's study (1994) bear a strong resemblance to the relationship styles identified by Hetherington (1988). In addition, Hetherington identified a fourth relationship style: the enmeshed sibling relationship. She terms this an enmeshed relationship "since it seemed to be a pathologically intense, symbiotic, and restrictive relationship" (1988:326). According to the author, enmeshed siblings are usually girls who are in divorced or remarried families and in families in which the child has no regular contact with an affectionate and involved adult.

To summarize, family factors are strongly involved in the quality of sibling relationships. These family factors are *differential parental behavior, the emotional climate of the family*, and *quality of the marital relationship*. Through their behavior toward their children and the quality of their marital relationship, parents can elicit rivalry among their offspring or foster sibling solidarity.

Sibling Solidarity and Rivalry across Cultures

According to Cumming and Schneider (1961), sibling solidarity is generally seen as one of the features of American kinship. People who lack siblings are inclined to describe their friends in terms of kinship compared to those who do have siblings. Cumming and Schneider also conclude that the sibling bond serves as a fundamental axis of emotional interaction. American kinship 'norms' regarding adult siblings include friendliness, family reunions, and sociability but do not include services or financial aid, although it may be necessary to help one's sibling(s) on occasion.

The ideal of sibling solidarity is certainly not confined to western industrialized societies. Themes of family solidarity and sibling solidarity are universals in the Mediterranean region. Yet, these norms are often contradicted by hostility and violence, primarily among brothers. For example, in Morocco, enmity between brothers and occasional fratricide are not uncommon (Gilmore 1982). In cultures that are focused on groups and families, such as Greece and Cyprus, as well as individualistic cultures, such as The Netherlands and Britain, strong emotional bonds between individuals and their family members are encouraged (Georgas, Christakopoulou, Poortinga, Angleitner, Goodwin and

Charalambous 1997). These authors found that family bonds (e.g., parent-child bonds, sibling bonds) vary more among individuals than between cultures. However, there are differences between adult sibling ties. One of the major differences is that in non-industrialized societies, sibling relationships tend to be obligatory whereas in industrialized societies, relationships among siblings tend to be discretionary; based on individual choice (see for an overview Cicirelli 1994).

The existing research on solidarity centers primarily on intergenerational solidarity. That is, solidarity between adult children and their parents (e.g., Lawton, Silverstein and Bengtson 1994; White and Rogers 1997). With few exceptions, solidarity between siblings growing up together is yet to be examined.

However, we do have two theoretical frameworks describing solidarity developed within sociology and social psychology, and an evolutionary perspective. In referring to Durkheim (organic and mechanical solidarity) and the social psychological literature on solidarity, while also drawing on Lewin (Field Theory), Homans, and Heider (Balance Theory), theoretical frameworks treat the family as small cohesive groups (McChesney and Bengtson 1988) in which the members are dependent upon each other. Durkheim coins this interdependency as organic solidarity and because people are interdependent they remain within the group. Heider brought in similarity of opinions or the importance of 'being on the same page', while Homans contributed by an emphasis on observable activities in small groups or what he calls "the things people do" ([1961] 1974:34).

Silverstein and Bengtson (1997) describe six principal dimensions of (intergenerational) solidarity: structure (e.g., geographic distance); association (e.g., frequency of social contact and shared activities); affect (e.g., feelings of emotional closeness); consensus; function (e.g., exchange of instrumental assistance and support); and norms (ideology of obligations). These six dimensions are operationalized conceptually in indicators of solidarity: frequency of contact, emotional closeness, similarity of opinions, geographic proximity, receiving instrumental assistance and providing instrumental assistance. These six manifest indicators of solidarity cluster into three groups that depict the concept of solidarity better than the original six principles. The first group is affinity (emotional closeness and consensus of opinions). The second group is opportunity structure since geographic proximity and frequency of contact are necessary conditions for exchange behavior. The third group is functional exchange: providing and receiving assistance. Silverstein's and Bengtson's research is one of few studies pertaining to solidarity and focuses on intergenerational solidarity among adult children-parents' relationships. House, Umberson and Landis (1988) refer to the family as a social network structure in which the structure has its effects through social support, social regulation, control, relational demands, and conflict.

From an evolutionary perspective, solidarity is described in terms of kin altruism and reciprocal altruism. Its focus is on inclusive fitness mechanisms. Kin altruism indicates altruism toward genetically related individuals and enhances one's own inclusive fitness. People are inclined to reciprocal altruism only if there are mutual benefits. Sulloway (1998) states that cooperation between unrelated individuals occurs as long as there are mutual benefits.

Sibling fights, conflicts, and rivalries are universal in both industrial and non-industrial societies despite the ideal of love, cooperation, and sharing. Sibling cooperation occurs when resources are limited, as is often the case in non-industrial societies. In ancestral environments solidarity is a means of survival of the family (Cicirelli 1995). This suggests that whenever there is a high degree of interdependence between family members, there is also a high degree of solidarity between those family members because they need each other. However, evolutionary psychology and socio-biological explanations of cooperation, solidarity, and altruism are theoretical explanations and are primarily tested experimentally in laboratory settings.

Sibling Relationships after Divorce and Remarriage

Most adults in the United States report their relationships with siblings as important and those relationships are characterized by feelings of closeness. Women tend to feel closer to their siblings than men regardless of the sex of the siblings; however, sibling relationships are affected by whether the family was intact or contained some combinations of stepsiblings or half siblings. Adults from intact families felt closer to all their siblings than adults who grew up in blended families (Pulakos 1990). This scholar notes that feelings of support and openness may be reflective of parents not showing favoritism and not interfering in sibling conflicts during earlier stages of childhood. Closeness among siblings is further influenced by marital status (the unmarried have more contact with their siblings) and gender (women function as 'kin-keepers'). In a study pertaining to social support among siblings, White and Riedmann (1992a) found that two-thirds of adults identified a sibling as close friend.

However, death of parents removes the linkage between adult brothers and sisters and divorce generally removes contacts with brothers-in-law and sisters-in-law. According to Rosenberg and Anspach, "each spouse serves as a connecting link between their consaguines and their own spouses. When that link is missing, so too is the continuity in kinship relations with one's affines" (1973:112). These authors conclude that divorce usually rekindles relationships with the blood related siblings: "sibling solidarity may be the one way that the kinship system becomes operative as a source of socio-emotional support when the conjugal relation is no longer intact" (1973:112).

What happens with sibling relationships when the siblings are children or adolescents in situations of divorce and remarriage? A growing number of children are not raised in a family constellation where both biological parents and full siblings are present. In 1995, only 50.8 percent (33.4 million) of school age children in the United States resided in such a family setting. Yet, this might even be an optimistic figure as one parent may be absent due to parental marital separation (ERS Staff Report 1995). Each year about 1.2 million couples divorce (Kreider and Fields 2001).

Parental divorce changes the family structure. The often conflict-laden relationship between the (divorced) mother and the father has an effect on the parent-child relationship. And although divorce does not make children fatherless, because of the physical separation of their parents children generally do not see their father as often as before the divorce, reflecting a gender imbalance in parenting. Booth and Amato found that twelve years after the divorce of their parents, respondents report less closeness with fathers. However, divorce is not the only contributing factor to lessened family cohesion: "Marital unhappiness and instability appear to weaken relationships between children and parents later in life, even if it does not result in divorce" (1994:31).

Spigelman, Spigelman and Englesson (1992) compared family drawings of, and conducted interviews with, 108 Swedish children from intact and divorced families. The divorced families had been divorced for an average of 6.9 years (range 3 months to 12 years) and the level of parental education was similar for both groups. Their study revealed that the number of children who omitted family members from their drawings was significantly higher in the divorce group suggesting that the child had a conflict-laden relationship with the omitted person. There was a tendency to omit the stepfather (when the mother remarried). Further, the figures drawn by children from divorced families tended to reflect negative emotions (e.g., sinister, sad, gloomy), whereas the figures drawn by children of intact families tended to have positive expressions (e.g., smiling, calm, happy). Drawings of boys from divorced families especially contained more negative and less positive expressions. Further, boys from divorced families had a greater tendency to omit full siblings and half siblings from their drawings than the other children. The authors suggest that this is possibly an indication of boys' more intensive sibling rivalry and of the greater impact of divorce and remarriage on boys than on girls.

Divorced mothers are less sensitive to their sons' needs than to their daughters' needs and give more negative and less positive feedback to their sons than to their daughters (Hetherington 1988). The son may resemble his biological father in physical appearance and/or the mother may see negative traits of the father in the son.

Stepfamilies have difficulties acquiring step-parenting skills (e.g., Bohannan and Erickson 1978; White and Gilbreth 2001). Further, status, duties, and privileges must be redefined, and solidarity in the new household must be reestablished. Positive sibling relationships are crucial to the success of stepfamilies. The better the relations between the blended sibling group, the better the total family integration (Skeen et al. 1984). When their stepfather is warm and sets limits, boys in blended families tend to function better than children in single parent families or conflicted non-divorced families. Stepfathers tend to have a positive effect on stepsons when these conditions are met (Bohannan and Erickson 1978).

MacKinnon (1989) investigated dyadic sibling interactions in married and divorced families and found that boys from divorced families are more aggressive, non-compliant, and impulsive than children from intact families. MacKinnon's study also revealed that sibling dyads containing older males within divorced families engage in highly abusive behavior such as nagging, hitting, and name-calling. Further, older males in divorced families were more negative towards their younger sister(s) than when the sibling dyad contained a younger brother. An explanation that was suggested by the author centers on the possibility that these boys 'mirror' the husband-wife structure (i.e., the conflicted relationship between their parents), which they witnessed prior to the divorce. An insensitive and/or punitive parenting style of the divorced mother may fuel conflict between siblings. According to MacKinnon (1989), this parenting style is likely to occur when the mother lacks support or assistance from her (ex) spouse. After their parents' divorce, children may seek allies among their siblings or form a coalition with another family member (Filinson 1986). However, coalitions are also formed in traditional nuclear families where, due to inter-parental conflict, mother-child coalitions are not uncommon (Kerig 1995). Kerig terms these 'triangular families'.

In a study pertaining to sibling relationships in a Mormon polygamous community, Jankowiak and Diderich (2000) found evidence that despite an ideology that fosters a harmonious family, siblings tend to display more solidarity toward their full siblings than toward their half siblings. In this community, siblings, through the guidance of their birthmother, tend to cluster around their birthmother's unit. It is assumed that polygamy promotes competition between co-wives, which is carried over into competition between their children (Schlegel and Barry 1991). These authors also suggest that competition between siblings over parental attention may be higher in traditional nuclear families than in other family forms. It is likely that children in traditional nuclear families feel safe and secure enough to express these feelings.

Summary

The vast majority of research on family relations has focused on traditional nuclear families. We know that full siblings have different personalities and develop different niches within their traditional nuclear family as a result of competition over limited parental resources. Parents have a dominant effect on their children's relationships; they can both elicit and mute solidarity and rivalry and thus influence the type of sibling relationship (e.g., harmonious, typical, conflicted) and have an impact on their children's emotional well being through differential parental treatment. In the United States, solidarity among full siblings is seen as a strong norm and usually siblings feel close to one another.

Protecting the family against extinction and thus benefiting close kin over more distant kin is satisfactorily explained by evolutionary theory and provides us with answers as to why, despite differences in personality, children display solidarity with their full siblings. Given the overemphasis on the traditional nuclear family and its decline, which leads to the formation of blended or remarried families, there are questions that remain yet unanswered. How is solidarity in a blended family established? Do children in blended families feel closer to their full siblings or to their half siblings or stepsiblings? What are the mechanisms underlying solidarity in contemporary American families? Is evolutionary theory useful in explaining part of the puzzle pertaining to solidarity in remarried families?

Given the fragmentation in psychological, sociological and anthropological literature, I suggest, in line with Berscheid (1995), a broader research view using all the sub-disciplines of the social sciences to describe and explain American family constellations. Along with evolutionary theory, family systems theory seems a fruitful theoretical framework to give us indications how to explain and describe family constellations and interactions.

Characteristics of sibling relationships are warmth and closeness, power and status, conflict and rivalry. In general, same-sex siblings tend to report warmth and closeness between them. Power and status play a role when the age difference between siblings is more than four years. More narrow-spaced siblings experience conflict in their relationship, and rivalry is more pronounced among younger siblings and in families with four or more children. Rivalries and conflict are natural among young children and may be a necessary condition for feelings of closeness with their siblings at a later age. In middle childhood, children develop a need for privacy and claim jurisdiction over their own space. Firstborn and lastborn children are the children who are likely to be the beneficiaries of their parent's investments.

Personality differences between siblings are attributed to the within family environment. In other words, children's personalities are shaped within their family, which makes this study even more interesting since children grow up in a succession of different family constellations in which their guiding principle is to avoid inequitable treatment. Children want to be treated equitably as compared to their full siblings present within their family, and may likely demand equitable treatment as compared to half siblings and stepsiblings. When a biological parent plays favorites or invests more in the offspring of his or her spouse, this is likely to evoke problems within the remarried family. From an evolutionary theory perspective, a husband would be interested in having as many children as he can, being interested in quantity, and thus sire children with his new wife. The wife in the remarried family would be interested in quality. That is, she would prefer to have investments in her children instead of investments in the children produced in her husband's previous marriage, while at the same time, for reasons of depicting her family as a harmonious family, she may feel an obligation to promote solidarity between her 'old' and 'new' family.

We now also know that, in general, women tend to feel closer to their siblings than men. Sisters who are full siblings may develop an enmeshed sibling relationship when their parents divorce. Nevertheless, divorce seems to have a more negative impact on boys since they may express negativity toward their younger sister, possibly imitating their father's behavior in the years prior to the marriage dissolution. In addition, those boys may develop conflict-laden relationships with other family members, such as their siblings, since omitting siblings and other family members from family drawings is a clear indication thereof. Remarriage may be beneficial for male children since it provides a male role model within the household. However, it is only beneficial if their stepfather is a warm and caring adult who sets limits.

Children may or may not be thrilled by their residential parent's decision to remarry. If they are receptive, it is likely that they are inclined to develop relationships with their step and half siblings that resemble friendship-type relationships. However, parental favoritism can undermine their children's intentions. If children would rather stay in a single parent household, in the case of remarriage, I suspect that they may sabotage this remarriage by forming alliances with their full siblings and create an 'us versus them' family environment. Another strategy, which is age related, is withdrawal from their new family. Teenagers who are at the brink of going to college and moving away from home may simply not care and thus not invest in their new family members. This may reflect the applicability of rational choice models.

The 'dilution hypothesis' seems fruitful in explaining rivalries among larger sibling groups in remarried families. The more children present, the less time a parent has for each child. Since the concept of a remarriage is that two families are joined together, remarried families will usually consist of larger sibling groups than traditional nuclear families. In this situation, which is change that can be perceived as stressful, because children are confronted with new family members, social comparison processes are heightened in the early years of a remarriage and children will monitor how they and their siblings are treated, and they are guided by avoiding inequity and restoring equity. However, biological parents may be naturally inclined to favor their own offspring, thus provoking rivalries and negative relationships among their blended sibling group.

CHAPTER FOUR
Methods of Sociological Inquiry

This chapter describes the methodology of the study, the rationale for choice of research methods, time of data collection, justification of the use of secondary data sets, and choice of methods for analyses. The chapter also provides a description of critiques on previous studies pertaining to remarried families, as well as an in-depth examination of the usefulness of a triangulation of research methods in family research.

This study relies on three sources of (qualitative and quantitative) data: observations in a series of 'Blended Family Workshops' in order to gain a better understanding of the problems that arise in remarried families; a 'Family of Orientation' assignment in which college students reflect upon their family of orientation and the siblings who are part of that family; and three waves of the General Social Survey which provide data pertaining to family cohesion and sibling solidarity.

I examine family ties in remarried families, problems in the initial stages of being part of a blended family, as well as the levels of solidarity among blended sibling groups. I investigate the levels of functional solidarity, associational solidarity, normative solidarity, and affectual solidarity among full siblings, half siblings and stepsiblings. The study specifically addresses the following hypotheses: In general, I expect to find: 1A) more functional solidarity between full siblings than between half siblings and stepsiblings; 1B) more associational solidarity between full siblings than between half siblings and stepsiblings; 1C) more affectual solidarity between full siblings than between half siblings and stepsiblings; 2) The greater the opportunity for interaction (e.g., living together), the greater the level of solidarity among siblings (functional, affectual, associational); 3) Siblings of the same gender and who are close in age will display more solidarity between them than siblings who differ in these ways; 4) Married siblings will display less solidarity with their siblings than unmarried (never married, divorced and widowed) siblings.

The next section outlines the mainstream approach to (remarried) families which, according to feminist scholars, overemphasizes a positivist manner of sociological inquiry (a quantitative focus on white nuclear middle class families) to the detriment of family diversity that may be better addressed with qualitative research.

Feminist Critiques on Methods of Sociological Inquiry

In 1974, Dorothy Smith outlined that objective knowledge as claimed by sociologists is not possible. Sociological research is always situated in a context. Therefore, sociologists must reveal where they stand with their methodological and theoretical framework ([1974] 1999). Feminist Katherine Allen (2000) is straightforward in her rejection of positivist science. She argues that a positivist science is not appropriate for studying the diversity of families in contemporary society. The notion of objectivity is obsolete since objectivity is often used as a shield behind which people in positions of power hide in order to shape the discourse and practice in family studies. However, she notes, who we are in the world shapes our statements regarding the work we do. Allen acknowledges that the dominant discourse on family studies in mainstream academic journals is still positivist and thus biased. In her view, there is no such thing as value-free science. Identities, feelings, and ideologies that should be part of the discourse are left out in the positivist objective report that is a result of inquiry.

Furthermore, scholars have focused solely on the traditional nuclear white middle class family and excluded the variety of family constellations in contemporary American society. Because subjective elements are left out in our research findings, we create false oppositions and "sustain these constructions as if they were real things that could be categorized and prioritized, as in male is better than female, White is better than Black" (Allen 2000:6).

Fox and Murray (2000) recognize four characteristics that are common to feminist approaches in research: reflexivity, action oriented research, praxis, and rethinking paradigms. First, there is reflexivity in scholarship. We have to recognize that we are actors involved in the generation of knowledge. Through reflexivity we know that we can learn more about the author's interpretation and how to evaluate the scholarship if we know more about why and how the knowledge was created. We must be willing to engage in conscious self-criticism and question our own biases towards our research topic. We must empower our subjects of study rather than exploit them, as is the case in 'academic colonialism'. We need to broaden our subject base with families of color. In this regard, Lasch discusses the Moynihan report which resulted in a shift in attention from racism and poverty to the false assumption of the black matriarchal family (Lasch [1977] 1999).

Second, we must put practice central. We must recognize that our research about the structures and processes, which are at the roots of inequality, are political in nature. We must contribute to reshaping existing social conditions toward greater equality for both men and women. Since feminist scholars are concerned with the lives of women, this concern must be reflected in our choice of topics.

Third, our focus is on process. We are concerned with the social processes through which patterns of inequality are generated, are sustained over time, and how they reproduce themselves. Life is an ongoing continuous process, which cannot be artificially divided into different compartments. Feminist research is always action-oriented as it seeks to change inequitable structures.

Fourth, we must rethink our paradigms. Knowledge is always a product of the producer. Until recently, knowledge was produced by those who had power. We have to include women's experiences and recognize that men and women speak different languages. According to feminist scholars, we have been listening to men for centuries since men traditionally dominated the sciences. The failure to recognize the different realities in women's lives and the failure to hear their different voices stems in part from a single mode of research, which is outlined in the positivist paradigm.

Fox and Murray (2000) note that family studies assume gender and race neutrality. In research, the same measurement is used for men, women, Whites and Blacks. Therefore, our knowledge base is problematic because large national scale survey data sets mistakenly presume gender and race neutrality. According to these authors, conflicts and arguments are interpreted differently by men and women and we thus make mistakes in the interpretations of our data.

This particular research project therefore relies on three sources of data. First, I discuss qualitative research and the rationale for participant observation in a 'Blended Family Workshop'. Second, I describe, the methodology behind the 'Family of Orientation', which is both qualitatively and quantitatively oriented. Third, I provide justification for the use of three waves of the General Social Survey and describe background information pertaining to these data sets. The next section addresses qualitative research and its benefits for this particular study.

Qualitative Research

Qualitative research is an umbrella term for a variety of research methods aimed at gathering and analyzing qualitative data such as: ethno methodology, in-depth interviews, content analysis, participant observation and grounded theory methods.

Inductive propositions in qualitative research develop as the researcher goes into the field with abstract notions. During the process of data collection there is continuous interaction between the data gathered and the theoretical notions that develop, they get more refined, and the researcher may decide to follow another path of sociological inquiry. The process is a continuous going back and forth between the data and the concepts as they develop (Neuman 2000).

We use the results in a manner that they contribute to generating middle range theories or contribute to a part of 'grand' theories. This inductive approach is characterized as "you begin with detailed observations of the world and move toward more abstract generalization and ideas. When you begin, you may only have one topic and a few vague concepts. As you observe you refine the concepts, develop empirical generalizations, and identify preliminary relationships. You build the theory from the ground up" (Neuman 2000:49).

According to Hammersley (1989), who expands on previous work by sociologist Blumer, sociological inquiry and analytic induction are explorations that may rely on a variety of research strategies (e.g., observation, interviews, and life histories). A researcher may have vague or abstract notions in the beginning of the research project and adapt a flexible attitude. He or she may shift from one line of inquiry to another and adopt new points of view as the study develops. Ultimately, he or she will acquire more information and have a better understanding of the topic of study. Certain generalizations can be made to similar contexts based on the concepts that have been developed during the research project.

Charmaz articulates these processes as outlined in grounded theory as: "Grounded theory methods consist of systematic inductive guidelines for collecting and analyzing data to build middle-range theoretical frameworks that explain the collected data" (2000:509). The researcher takes a dialectic approach as he or she is in continuous interaction with data interpretation, further data collection and refining the theoretical analysis. Grounded theory aims to specify relationships between concepts in a theoretical explanatory framework (Dey 1999). Charmaz explains that grounded theory methods "move each step of the analytical process toward the development, refinement, and interrelation of concepts" (2000:510).

Conventionally, grounded theory assumes an objective, external reality and a neutral observer who discovers the data using the guidelines previously discussed. Results yielded through grounded theory are evaluated using four criteria: fit, work, relevance, and modifiability. Theoretical categories must fit the data collected; every case study has to fit in. Grounded theory must provide a useful conceptual framework that explains the phenomena studied. The relevance of these phenomena is reflected in the analytic explanations of problems in the research setting. Lastly, grounded theory is flexible in the way that a researcher can modify the established analysis when conditions change or more data are gathered. Grounded theorists usually employ a triangulation of methods such as in-depth interviews and participant observation, ensuring that the topic of study is accurately represented and that findings can be generalized to similar contexts (Neuman 2000).

Some critics argue that grounded theorists dissect their data too much; they aim for analysis rather than depicting the subjects' experience fully. They 'cram' data in categories, thus reducing the richness of the data. Other scholars accuse grounded theorists of manipulating data, such as choosing evidence selectively, cleaning up statements of interviewees, and adoption of value-laden metaphors (for an overview see Charmaz 2000:521-522). Because of these critiques, Charmaz pleads for a modification of grounded theory in the form of constructivist grounded theory. The latter would use the methods as developed by grounded theory and also move into the realm of interpreting the social world without assuming the existence of an external, objective and true reality. Instead, the focus is on interpretation and reflexivity. Marshall and Rossman address problems with generalization of qualitative studies in general. They state, "Within the parameters of the setting, population and theoretical framework, the research will be valid" (1989:145). However, transferability or demonstrating the applicability of the findings to another context is entirely up to the researcher.

Jorgensen (1989) views participant observation and in-depth interviews as excellent research tools in particular settings. For example, "when a phenomenon is somewhat obscured from the view of outsiders (private intimate interaction and groups)", or "the phenomenon is hidden from the public view", or "little is known about the phenomenon", or when "there are important differences between the views of insiders as opposed to outsiders" (1989:12-13). There are certain minimal conditions that need to be present in order to justify participant observation. These conditions include that "the research problem is concerned with human meanings and interactions viewed from the insiders' perspective", "that the phenomenon of investigation is observable within an everyday life situation or setting", and that "the researcher is able to gain access to an appropriate setting" (1989:13). Jorgensen further states that research is "about human life grounded in the realities of daily existence" (1989:14).

Following Jorgensen's guidelines, whether or not used in conjunction with grounded theory, a researcher will be able to accurately represent the object of study and will, due to theoretical truths, be able to generalize to similar contexts or settings. In reporting the data, a researcher must provide us with essential method talk. How did he or she gain access to an object of study? How did he or she build rapport with the objects of study? What is the researcher's personal experience? Jorgensen notes "personal experience derived from direct participation in the insider's world is an extremely rich source of information, especially if the researcher has performed membership roles and otherwise experienced life as an insider" (1989:93).

Triangulation of methods and reflexivity on the researcher's part will enhance an accurate description and analysis of the topic studied. Representation is thus more likely. However, it is not easy to generalize findings to other contexts. In order to do so the researcher must justify that the theoretical concepts derived from the particular study are also applicable to other settings. Therefore, the data collection in my research project relies on three different sources and settings, representing different stages in the life course, which will make generalizations to the larger population somewhat more feasible.

Given Jorgensen's (1989) conditions and guidelines outlined by Dey (1999) and Charmaz (2000), participant observation in a 'Blended Family Workshop' is an appropriate research method for investigating problems that remarried families encounter. The participant observation is aimed at gaining an understanding of these issues. According to Neuman, it is a purposive sample, which is also a theoretical sample since it "gets cases that will help reveal features that are theoretically important about a particular setting/topic" (2000:196). The sample is a self-selective (non probability) sample, thus generalization to the entire population of remarried families is not feasible. However, this sample contributes to the development of theoretical concepts pertaining to remarried families. It is to be expected that participants in the workshop are aware of their problems and will talk freely about them, which in other contexts may be 'swept under the carpet'. Participant observation is a method for acquiring rich data and will give a better theoretical understanding of the issues in remarried families, although not necessarily every remarried family faces the same issues.

Blended Family Workshops

In order to explore the everyday reality of remarried families, which in other settings may be obscured from the view of the outsider, I sought participation in the 'Blended Family Workshop'. In a metropolitan area in the Southwest, the Department of Family Services (Parenting Project) offers workshops pertaining to blended families. The goal is to provide adults who have become parents in remarried families with opportunities to recognize and resolve problems that may occur in this type of family constellation. A person who marries someone who has been previously married often acquires a spouse and stepchildren, who may or may not reside in the household. Every adult who is part of a blended family can participate in this workshop.

In order to gain a better understanding of the problems that may arise in this type of family, I requested participation, primarily as an observer, in this workshop, which was granted. At the request of the participants, I was asked not to use a tape recorder, but instead take notes during the workshops. Field notes were written immediately following each workshop. The 'Blended Family Workshop' was organized as a series of four workshops in the fall of 2004. Each session lasted two to two and a half hours. Participants made a commitment to attend every workshop. Unlike other programs organized by the Department of Family Services, this particular workshop was on a voluntary basis rather than court ordered participation.

The moderator clarified my presence during the first workshop. I was introduced as someone who had a scholarly interest in the topic and participants were told that my participation would contribute to the manuscript that I was writing on blended families. Participants were given ample opportunity to address questions pertaining to my presence. I emphasized anonymity and confidentiality in reporting my findings. During the workshops I participated as much as was possible, given that I was raised in a traditional nuclear family and thus had no personal experience with remarried families. Participants expressed happiness about my presence. They thought it was valuable that researchers were interested in remarried families and their situation in particular.

During the four sessions, the following topics were discussed: stepfamily living, parenting styles (utilizing Diana Baumrind's 1966 and 1967 studies on styles of parenting), and children in blended families (session 1); stepfamily characteristics, becoming a confident stepparent, family rules (session 2); family communication, expectations in blended families, stress management, problem solving (session 3); myths and realities, stepfamily meetings, behavior management strategies, and stepfamily traditions (session 4). The moderator distributed flyers pertaining to the several topics. A total of five persons, two males and three females, participated in the workshop sessions: two couples in blended families and one woman seriously dating a man who had a son from a previous marriage were present. The latter person participated in the workshop because she wanted to know what potential problems could occur in her near future as a stepmother. Chapter five details my findings.

Family of Orientation Project

Another exploratory study was conducted with freshmen at a University in the Southwest of the United States of America. This particular study can be considered as a mix of a qualitative method and a quantitative method. Students who enrolled in two sections of a 101 'Principles of Sociology' class in the fall of 2004 were asked to submit an assignment pertaining to their family of orientation for which they would receive 5 credits. The main purpose of the assignment was to have them reflect on their family life, and to apply and relate sociological concepts to their family. They were told in advance that if they felt uncomfortable writing about their family, they could decline to write this particular assignment and, instead, could submit a paper about a different sociological topic. No student declined. The students obtained the assignments after lectures about the sociology of family and after a discussion of the corresponding chapter in their textbook. Students were given three weeks to complete the assignment.

Dillman (1978) who developed the 'Total Design Method', which is based on principles of social exchange, proposes to carefully identify each aspect of the survey process that may affect response quality and quantity. In order to reduce the risk of respondent's refusal to participate, there has to be a benefit or reward for the respondent, which must justify his costs (it must be worth the time that he or she spends on the survey). A reward can have a financial or an emotional value. The rewards of participation must be maximized and the cost must be minimized in order to get a respondent to participate and to complete the survey. For example, it can be rewarding for a student to write the 'Family of Orientation' assignment because he or she will get extra credit, and it can be a rewarding experience to reflect and write about one's family.

The assignment required students to submit a maximum of two pages in addressing the following four questions: 1) How would you describe the type of family you grew up in?; 2) Did you grow up with siblings? If yes, how many?; 3) Do you have any half or stepsiblings?; 4A) Who is your favorite sibling?; 4B) Why?

As follows, this particular sample is an opportunity or convenience sample. Only students enrolled in two sections of a 'Principles of Sociology' class had the opportunity to participate. Nevertheless, their answers provided rich information about their families of origin and their motivation in choosing a particular sibling as their favorite sibling.

Open-ended questions in this assignment are post-coded in several categories on a nominal level. For example, a question regarding the favorite sibling can be coded as: 1) male 2) female, and as 1) oldest 2) middle 3) youngest, and further as 1) full sibling 2) half sibling 3) stepsibling. Also, a question regarding the type of family can be coded as 1) traditional nuclear family 2) single parent family 3) blended family 4) divorced family 5) extended family 6) other type of family.

Testing for significance varies per measurement level. Data measured on nominal levels require Chi square tests and confidence intervals. Data on an ordinal level are tested with the appropriate tests for this level such as Spearman's r or Kendall's Tau. Data measured on an interval level and ordinal level require T-tests.

Quantitative Research

In order to gather data from a large sample size a researcher has the following realistic options: mail surveys, face-to-face interviews, phone surveys and secondary datasets. This section and the following section outline the benefits of the secondary datasets that I selected.

Neuman justifies the use of secondary datasets in articulating: "Any topic on which information has been collected and is publicly available can be studied. In fact, existing statistics projects may not fit neatly into a deductive model of research design. Rather, researchers creatively reorganize the existing information into the variables for a research question after first finding what data are available (2000:301).

In the study, I use a dataset (General Social Survey) that is available through the Inter-university Consortium for Political and Social Research (ICPSR). I extract those variables that have a close resemblance to the conceptual framework of family solidarity developed by Bengtson and Roberts (1991) and Silverstein and Bengtson (1997).

Their typology focuses on six forms of solidarity of which I use five forms: functional solidarity, affectual solidarity, associational solidarity, structural solidarity, and normative solidarity. Functional solidarity depicts the degree of helping and exchange of resources. Affectual solidarity represents the type and degree of positive sentiments held about siblings. Associational solidarity depicts the frequency and patterns of interaction in various types of activities in which siblings engage and is measured by questions that deal with shared activities of siblings. Structural solidarity measures the residential propinquity of family members and therefore reflects co-residence. Some researchers argue that co-residence will automatically lead to more solidarity between children; others argue that co-residence, as a special form of proximity, by the same token can elicit negative feelings and withdrawal from the family (White and Rogers 1997). Co-residence is therefore included as a control variable as well as age, gender and genetic relatedness of the siblings.

The investment of parents in their remarried family is reflected in their beliefs about a cohesive family unit. However, beliefs are not necessarily translated into actual behavior. According to Frey (1989) actual behavior is a better indicator than beliefs. Bengtson and Roberts describe it as normative solidarity or strength of commitment to meeting familial obligations.

General Social Survey

The General Social Survey (GSS) has been conducted since 1972. It is a nationally representative face-to-face interview survey of non-institutionalized adults in United States households held annually and, in later years (since 1994) held every other year by the National Opinion Research Center (NORC). The survey covers a broad variety of topics such as political and religious views and attitudes, beliefs about abortion, the family and social support networks. It also encompasses variables pertaining to demographics and household composition. The biennial survey has a split sample design, which consists of two parallel sub-samples of approximately 1,500 cases each. The sub-samples have identical core sets of questions, and two different topical modules. The 1994 General Social Survey, for example, covers the topical modules 'Family Mobility' and 'Multiculturalism'. There are currently 10 topical modules and two International Social Survey Program (ISSP) modules.

The General Social Survey has a high response rate of 70 to 75 percent during the last decades. The sampling frame, interviewer training and management of data collection are carefully constructed and monitored. More than 150 social scientists are involved in survey construction and administration procedures of the General Social Survey Series. NORC ensures that each General Social Survey sample is a national probability sample.

Currently, thirty years of the General Social Survey (1972-2002) are available in a cumulative data file, which has more than 43,000 respondents (N = 43,698) and 4,200 variables. I obtained this cumulative file through the Inter-university Consortium for Political and Social Research (ICPSR), which is located in Ann Arbor, Michigan. More than 1,000 of the questions have been replicated and

ICPSR claims that it has pooled "subgroups together into larger samples suitable for analysis" (http://webapp.icpsr.umich.edu/GSS/about/gss/about.htm).

For the purposes of this research project, I use several subsets to answer the research questions. Data about the genetic relationship between siblings (full, adopted, half and step) were only gathered in 1994. These particular data can thus only be used with other variables that were also measured in 1994. Three variables in the 1994 General Social Survey pertain to solidarity and are described in chapter five. Data gathered in 1986 and 2002 did not address the level of genetic relatedness to siblings. Thus, when respondents were asked about their siblings, they gave the total number of siblings (not broken down in number of full siblings, half siblings and stepsiblings). I use the 1994 data on siblings because research questions about solidarity can be addressed. Further, I also use data from the 1986 ('Social Support and Networks') and 2002 ('Social Networks') General Social Survey that later have been compiled in the 2001 ISSP module 'Social Relations and Support Systems' to answer research questions about sibling solidarity and family cohesion.

I provide basic descriptive analysis for demographic variables. Data measured on nominal and ordinal levels are analyzed by Chi-square tests. The effects of control variables (i.e., age, marital status, sex, proximity) on the different dependent variables are addressed by ordinary least squares (OLS) regression analysis. Finally, analysis of variance (ANOVA) is employed to establish whether there are significant differences between certain groups of siblings (i.e., full siblings, half siblings, stepsiblings, same sex siblings, cross-sex siblings, small age difference, large age difference) and their scores on sibling solidarity items.

The General Social Survey subsets, used in conjunction with data gathered in the 'Blended Family Workshop' and data obtained through the 'Family of Orientation' Assignment, address the research questions posed in this particular study. The results follow in the next chapter.

CHAPTER FIVE
Results

Because this project employs a triangulation of methods, I will discuss the results per method. First, the Blended Family Workshops are discussed, and then the assignment pertaining to Family of Orientation is addressed. The third section of this chapter details the analyses and results of the General Social Survey. This sequence reflects the order in which the data was gathered.

Findings from the Blended Family Workshops

The moderator of the workshops stressed that stepfamilies are different from biological families in many ways: stepfamilies are larger and more complex; they are born out of loss; every individual has a previous family history; children are members of two households; there is a biological parent elsewhere with influence and power in actuality or in memory; and a stepfamily initially lacks a sense of unity. A person, who marries someone with one or more children, is suddenly thrown into the role of stepparent without time to adjust gradually to the parenting role. However, it takes time to become a confident stepparent and the advice given is to go slowly and to act as a good role model. Further, for stepparents the adagio is to detach themselves and avoid emotional involvement, act nonchalant. In this respect, Ihinger-Tallman and Pasley (1997) note that less cohesion in the beginning is healthy for a well functioning remarried family later. These scholars note that it takes between three and five years for stepfamilies to develop a sense of cohesion and thus achieve family integration, that is, integration of each member in his or her family.

According to the workshop, problems experienced by the adult(s) with the child or children may have nothing to do with being a stepparent but everything to do with the child's developmental stage. This information was a relief for participants because they had attributed blame on themselves for problems with stepchildren.

Children respond differently to the divorce of their biological parents. That difference is not so much rooted in personality as it is in developmental stages of the children. Their reactions to divorce and remarriage are age related. Thus, it is not the presence of the stepparent, but the age-appropriate reactions of the child that should be known. It is important that the (step)parent recognizes this and frames the child's reaction in its appropriate context because the reactions of the child need not to be taken personally. For example, a four-year old may display behavior such as swearing, hitting and kicking and may display a wide range of feelings, where an eleven-year old might be prone to emotional outbursts. This behavior is not due to the presence of a stepparent but is considered normal behavior for a child in this stage and in this culture. Common childhood reactions to their parents' divorce range from sadness and a feeling of abandonment (pre-school children) to anger, disgust and confusion (14-year olds and 15-year olds).

Another issue that participants reflected upon is parenting style. What are participants' parenting styles (authoritarian, authoritative or permissive) and where do these styles stem from? We tend to repeat what is familiar and to practice what we have learned ourselves and with which we are comfortable. Regardless of type of family, "children appear to do best, when parents are warm and supportive, spend generous amounts of time with children, monitor children's behavior, expect children to follow rules, encourage open communication, and react to misbehavior with discussion rather than harsh punishment" (Amato and Fowler 2002:704).

What can be expected of elementary-aged children? They go through different ages and thus different stages. Insight into developmental stages of children and teenagers (ages one to 16) and parenting styles give indications about (step)parent-child interactions. For example, an 11-year old is starting to break away from parental influence and may challenge parents' views. Several flyers given to the participants provide a wealth of information on how to approach and deal with school age children. It is stressed that parenting is behavior; it is an active verb. Whether the parent is a stepparent or biological parent does not make a difference.

Common issues for children living in remarried families are: being blamed for everything that goes wrong, adjusting to new rules from the stepparent, and having stepbrothers or stepsisters mess with your things (Flyer Blended Families Workshop).

When people form a blended family it is helpful for family unity and cohesion to implement family rules and stepfamily meetings, and to create stepfamily traditions. Family rules are guidelines that clarify which behavior is acceptable and which is not and what is expected of family members. The family rules apply to everybody (e.g., clean up after yourself, no yelling; when you hear yourself yell move closer to the particular person). Young children benefit from rules for specific times of the day (e.g., quiet time at a certain hour, snack time at a certain hour). Stepfamily meetings are encouraged, and they should be brief (20 to 30 minutes) and regularly scheduled meetings. Their purpose is to encourage understanding and to foster cooperation. They center on shared decision-making, allowing family members 'to be on the same page'. Stepfamily traditions are routines unique to a family such as Saturday afternoon board games, going to church every Sunday morning, Sunday afternoon movies, or Wednesday night suppers. One of the challenges for remarried families, as noted by Mary Whiteside (1989), is that there are few societal guidelines for organizing these types of families in kinship systems.

Family rituals, focusing on traditions, and everyday interactions, are important keys to kinship connections. During family celebrations, connections in the remarried family supra system (or the extended kin network) are established.

Whiteside states that different areas of ritual performance reinforce different levels of family identity (i.e., the stepfamily household, the binuclear family and the family supra system). In her view, "interactions on the level of daily routines are critical in the development of stepfamily cohesion...." (1989:37). Stepfamilies may eventually function as nuclear families. Whiteside elaborates: "For those families who successfully substitute stepkin for the nonresident biological parent's kin, kinship patterns and family rituals would be expected to more closely resemble patterns of nuclear families at all levels of ritual" (1989:39).

During the workshops, there are also suggestions for what a parent can do with children and how to bond with them on an age-appropriate level. Part of the bonding process between (step)parent and child is reading books to children. Other suggestions are to help with homework and to show an interest in the child's hobbies. One participant voiced her distress about other people commenting on her family. Her stepsons resembled their biological mother who was of a different race. It was therefore assumed that the stepmother was an adoptive parent. For the outside world she wanted her family to be perceived as a 'normal' family. For her 'normal' meant a traditional nuclear family with a husband and wife and their biological offspring. Since it was apparent that the children did not resemble her, this was not the case. She felt that this made bonding with her stepchildren, which she desired, more challenging and difficult. Apparently, physical similarity between stepparent and stepchildren facilitates the bonding process.

Another issue brought up by the same person was that she wished when tucking them in for the night she could tell these children 'I love you'. She struggled because she couldn't; she would feel like a hypocrite. Apparently she was stuck between wanting to love these stepchildren and her own feelings about them. It caused her much grief as was demonstrated by her tearful outbursts. After school, the younger stepchild would follow her around, offering help with errands. This child was seemingly seeking opportunities to communicate and make contact and bond with the new mother. Ambivalence about family members (e.g., loving your stepsons when you don't know them yet) and ambiguity about the stepparent role are theoretical concepts derived from participant observation during the workshops.

In a remarried family, it takes time to get to know your family members and to grow to love them. However, it is important in stepparent-stepchild relationships to note that stepfamily adjustment is fostered, and marital satisfaction increases when the relationship between those stepfamily members is mutually satisfying. Whether the relationship is warm or detached does not matter, as long as both parties involved are satisfied with it (Ihinger-Tallman and Pasley 1997).

During the workshops, myths about blended families are debunked and realities are introduced. For example, one myth is that "children whose parents are divorced can be expected to suffer behavior problems and problems in schools" (Flyer Blended Family Workshop). The reality is that "Any change in the family structure can result in temporary behavior problems. These problems only become permanent when they are reinforced." Therefore, parenting is the key to preventing problems and time is devoted to parenting behavior and the developmental stages of the child or children. Continuous arguments between parent and child can be avoided by starting sentences with 'nevertheless' and 'regardless' and by using phrases such as 'That won't work for me'. It is advised that parents avoid power struggles and choose battles carefully.

A couple participating in the workshop voiced their distress pertaining to step-fathering her child and step-mothering his child. The origin of the distress was rooted in an inability to bond with the new partner's child and a genuine desire to treat both children the same. Hetherington (2003), an authority on family processes, offers a suggestion for parents when she states: "In all types of families, authoritative parents who are warm, supportive, communicative and responsive to their children's needs, and who exert firm, consistent and reasonable control and close supervision, provide a positive environment for the healthy and competent development of children" (p. 228). However, the remarried family is a family system that is inherently different from the traditional nuclear family in terms of supervision, acceptance and the granting of autonomy. In traditional nuclear families these concepts are hierarchically organized with the mother providing the most supervision, acceptance and decisions regarding autonomy, then the father and then an older sibling. In remarried families those concepts are non-hierarchical (Kurdek and Fine 1995). These authors further suggest an important role for older siblings as socialization agents for their younger counterparts in remarried families.

Individuals in stepfamilies need time to each adjust to their new role in this type of family. One stepmother had a baby, her stepchildren's half sibling. The 10-year old stepchild wanted to help and offered to take care of the baby on Sunday mornings so the stepmother, who was sleep-deprived, could sleep in. Other than pleasing the stepmother, a reward in itself, it also provides the child with an opportunity to bond with his baby half sibling. Nevertheless, adding an 'our' child to the family should not be done to cement bonds between marital partners. The cultural myth that 'having a baby strengthens a marital relationship' does not hold true for first marriages and is not applicable to remarriages either. Instead, "Remarried couples who bear children add further complexity to an already complicated system" (Ganong and Coleman 1988:689). These scholars found no differences between remarried families with mutual children and remarried families without mutual children when they used several scales regarding family feelings and quality of dyadic (spousal) interaction.

People participating in these workshops were highly motivated to become good stepparents and contribute to family unity; they took a real interest in their stepchildren and in blending their families. For the outside world they want to be perceived as any other 'normal family' which for them is the traditional nuclear family. One man in particular said he participated in these workshops to support his wife who was a stepmother to his two children. He said he realized how difficult it was for her and he appreciated her efforts. For him, participation in the workshops demonstrated his love for and commitment to his new wife and a determination to create a harmonious family. The notion of creating a harmonious family, the desire to be perceived as any other 'normal' family and to strive for family unity is a longing for family cohesion and thus normative solidarity. When people enter marriage for the first time, this longing for family cohesion is absent since the couple's focus is on adjusting to each other; they focus on the pair bond. In second and higher order marriages with children, the spouses become part of a family instantly and have to adjust to several family members and create family unity because they are family from the moment they enter wedlock.

Every relationship, according to Simmel, is characterized by balancing distance versus closeness. The dyad expands into a triad when a third individual is added and two separate units within this triad emerge: the parental unit and the child unit. The third party strengthens the parental unit because there is a common goal to provide for the child until it reaches maturity. In remarried or blended families this juggling of distance versus closeness may require a substantial amount of time before a satisfying balance is achieved. Notably, ambivalence is embedded in the social structure and conflict is normal. In stepfamilies, there exist multiple statuses and multiple roles (Bengtson et al. 2002). These scholars distinguish structural ambivalence, stemming from the individual's location in the social structure, and psychological ambivalence, referring to sentiments experienced by individuals when faced with structural ambivalence. They suggest that ambivalence emerges at the intersection of solidarity and conflict. They note: "...each shows us how family members attempt to stay together, what pulls them apart, and how to negotiate their differences" (Bengtson et al. 2002:575). Spouses and family members who are entering a higher order marriage may be ambivalent about their location in the social structure, thus heightening their psychological ambivalence as is nicely illustrated with the emotional torment that one of the stepmothers in the 'Blended Family Workshop' went through.

Luescher (2002), who traces the term ambivalence to psychiatrists Sigmund Freud and Eugen Bleuler, offers a sociological definition of the concept of ambivalence: "it is useful to speak of ambivalence when polarized simultaneous emotions, thoughts, social relations, and structures that are considered relevant for the constitution of individual or collective identities are (or can be) interpreted as temporarily or even permanently irreconcilable" (p. 587). According to Luescher, ambivalence is basic to the human condition and when connecting a (fragmented) self to the larger social structure in contemporary society, he remarks "postmodernism makes a strong point that the social world contains differences that can never be fully resolved, yet have to be lived with" (p. 591). Ambivalence is a precursor to both family harmony and family conflict.

Stepfamilies are prone to experiencing ambivalence and problems with establishing and maintaining boundaries. Ambivalence and Simmel's concept of closeness and distance have been applied to stepfamily research. Galvin, Bylund and Brommel state: "Between step-relations there is a tension between getting close and staying distant in order to remain loyal to a biological parent or child" (2004:72). Recently, scholars found that communication between stepparent and child is dominated by three concepts: integration (distance versus closeness), status (parent role and its legitimacy), and dialectic of expression (candor and discretion) (Baxter, Braithwaite and Wagner 2004).

Spouses and other members in a remarried family redefine family rules and roles. According to family systems theory, within a family exists a set of rules and regulations pertaining to the participating members. These regulations, specify, who, when and how members participate in family life. When a new remarried family is formed, the members experience uncertainty regarding their perceptions of who belongs to this family, and who is performing what tasks and roles within the family. This uncertainty in stepfamilies' is phrased as the 'unclear family' (Simpson 1998) whose members deal with what is labeled 'boundary ambiguity' (Pasley and Ihinger-Tallman 1989).

Lastly, it is observed during the Blended Family Workshops that gift giving by genetically unrelated kin (such as a stepson who offers to take care of the baby) might evoke feelings of uneasiness since there is an expectation to reciprocate sooner or later (reciprocal altruism). This expectation of needing to reciprocate after receiving a gift may be absent with genetically related kin (kin altruism).

Participant observation during the Blended Family Workshop thus contributed insights to theoretical notions of normative solidarity, ambivalence, ambiguity, bonding with new family members, and the notion of kin altruism and reciprocal altruism. The following section examines the results from the 'Family of Orientation' assignment

Findings from the Family of Orientation Project

A total of 215 students out of 244 or 88 percent turned in the assignment. Seventy-five males and 140 females participated. The data from those 215 first year students (collected in 2004) are used to give more qualitative information and quantitative information pertaining to siblings in remarried families.

A slight majority of students (N = 110 or 51 percent) describe their family of orientation as a traditional nuclear family. Thirty percent (N = 65) grew up in a remarried family constellation where one or both biological parents remarried. Eleven percent (N = 24) specifically state that their family of orientation was a divorced family (not remarried), while six students report growing up in a widowed family where one of the parents had died and the surviving parent had not remarried. Seven students were raised in a single-parent family constellation (never been married) and three students grew up in other types of families (i.e., in foster care, or with extended kin such as aunts and grandparents). Thus, the majority of students (N = 175 or 81 percent) were raised in a traditional nuclear family or in a bi-nuclear remarried family reflecting the diversity in family life in the contemporary United States. In the same year in which I collected my data (2004), 68 percent of children (between the ages of 0 and 17) lived in a household with two married parents (biological, adoptive and/or stepparent), according to national statistics (Federal Interagency Forum on Child and Family Statistics 2007). Thus, my sample is somewhat representative compared to national data (81 percent versus 68 percent respectively).

Seventeen respondents mistakenly identified their family of orientation as a traditional nuclear family while one of their parents had previously been married. In these instances, both biological parents were present and had been married to each other for more than twenty years. However, half siblings were present in the household and technically these families are remarried families although respondents may see it differently from their perspective since they were never confronted with a divorce or remarriage of either one of their parents. To them, their family is a traditional nuclear family. For the purpose of this research project, they were technically identified as remarried families.

Table 1.

Type of Family

Type of Family	Number	Percentage
Traditional Nuclear Family	110	51
Remarried Family	65	30
Divorced Family	24	11
Widowed Family	6	3
Single Parent Family	7	3
Other	3	1

Family

Respondents voiced an overwhelming happiness with their family of orientation whether it was the nuclear, bi-nuclear, single parent or divorced family. Many marveled at the benefits of the traditional nuclear family and the values it instills in their offspring:

> I strongly believe that a traditional nuclear family makes a person stronger not only in themselves but in each other. To have a good core to always fall back on helps so much in a person's life because they always have confidence that they have people to trust. (Female, traditional nuclear family)
>
> What makes my family the true "ideal family" is that my parents had two kids; one of each gender plus a few dogs, cats and also a little piglet along the way. (Female, traditional nuclear family)
>
> My family is absolutely wonderful. I love every single one of them so much and I know that I was really lucky to be put in a family with such strong values and solid beliefs. My family is the best. (18-year old female, traditional nuclear family)

One observant male compares his family favorably to other types of families as he notes:

> My family is normal by my standards. That is to say that I have only my friends' families to compare to. Most of my friends have moved out from home, have divorced parents and contain some small level of hatred, anger, or resentment towards one or both parents. (Male with two brothers)

In spite of multiplication of family structures over the life course in recent decades, adults still deal with notions of normalcy (personal communication with Karla Hackstaff 2008). The traditional nuclear family is still perceived by young adults ('Family of Orientation' assignment) and remarried adults (participating in a series of Blended Family Workshops) as the 'normal' and 'ideal' family.

Respondents raised in bi-nuclear families, having witnessed the divorce of their parents and the subsequent dating and remarriage of one or both of their parents, generally volunteer information about their families that is flattering. Talking about one's family evokes emotions, and a general attitude of gratitude as is articulated best by the following statements:

> My family has been a big part of my life. Even if we don't get along all the time, we love each other regardless of title and relation. We don't use half or step when we are talking about or to each other. (Female living with her dad and stepmother)

> A great number of people don't enjoy having what is known as mixed families or stepfamilies but I'm a bit different. I really do love both my step-parents even if they bother me at times. (Female in remarried family)

> As I have said before, I am lucky to have grown up in a family that radiates love and compassion. I would never change anything about the members of my bi-nuclear family. (Female with two full sisters, mother and stepfather)

> My family is absolutely perfect to me. Despite a divorce and a new mother entering my life, my family has been able to stay together happily and productively, and I am extremely thankful for being blessed with having such great people around me. (Female with one older brother, growing up in an extended family with grandparents – father remarried)

> I thank God every day to have such a wonderful family like I do, even if it is different from everyone else's. (Male in remarried family)

> But when you have a group of people together that are completely open, have no shame, and no boundaries, you probably have stumbled onto a family. And no matter how many times I may wish they weren't as odd as they are, they will always be my family. (Female from remarried family)

If I had a choice to change my family ties into a more 'normal' and 'acceptable' traditional family I would never in a million years. (Male with six half brothers and one half sister)

Again, the issue of normalcy is brought up as is the concept of boundaries within stepfamilies. Apparently, for the female who grew up in a remarried family, boundary and boundary ambiguity are issues in stepfamilies. Nevertheless, the point that emerges from these statements is that remarried families are not necessarily conflict-laden environments. Instead, remarried families can create a healthy environment and safe haven for children. Borrine and her colleagues Handal, Brown and Searight (1991) found that "remarriage, like divorce, is not a uniformly handicapping event for subsequent adolescent adjustment" (p. 754-755).

Siblings in Remarried Families

A frequency distribution shows that out of 65 respondents in remarried families, 52 percent of respondents (N = 34) chose their full sibling as their favorite sibling, 31 percent (N = 20) favored their half sibling and three percent favored their stepsibling. However, the question becomes: what are the choices? If a respondent has no full siblings and only half siblings, it is logical that a half sibling is picked as the favorite. Of the 65 individuals in remarried or bi-nuclear families, 18 respondents (or 28 percent) reported they did not have any constellation of full siblings, half siblings or stepsiblings and were therefore excluded from the analysis. The subset thus consisted of 47 respondents.

Of those 47, thirty-one respondents (66 percent) favored a full sibling, ten favored a half sibling (21 percent) and one favored a stepsibling. Thus, a majority of children growing up in remarried families favor a closer blood relative over someone with whom they have fewer genes in common. However, is this phenomenon a function of biology, cultural beliefs (about the importance of blood relatives) or a function of time and age? Children who grew up with each other from infancy may develop bonds with their half sibling(s) and stepsibling(s) similar to biological siblings. Seven respondents have no full siblings. Six of them prefer their half sibling to their stepsiblings while only one prefers the stepsibling to the half sibling. Omitting those seven respondents leaves us with 40 respondents.

Table 2.

Remarried Family and Preferred Sibling

Remarried Family	FS	HS	SS	No choice
All (N=65)	34	20	2	9
Any Mixture of Siblings (N=47)	31	10	1	5
No Full Siblings (N=7)		6	1	
One Full Sibling Present (N=25)	18	3	0	4
Two or More Full Siblings Present (N=15)	13	1	1	
One or More Full Siblings Present (N=40)	31	4	0	5

When one or more full siblings are present, thirty-one of forty respondents (78 percent) prefer a full sibling over half siblings and stepsiblings. Only four respondents favor a half sibling (10 percent) when full siblings are present, and five respondents indicate they have no preference.

When only one full sibling is present, the same pattern emerges. Eighteen out of 25 respondents (72 percent) favor their full sibling. Only three prefer a half sibling to a full sibling. Four respondents did not want to identify a favorite sibling.

None of the respondents has a stepsibling as the favorite sibling. Favoring one sibling over the other apparently follows this pattern: when no full siblings are present, half siblings are preferred; when a choice exists, full siblings are preferred as is articulated by the following statements which reflect a strong belief in biology:

> The cliché goes that family is family; however, in my eyes blood is blood, so this makes my older sister my favorite. (Male favoring his full sibling over his two half siblings)

> I would have to say I like my half sister the best. I never considered her my half sister and more like a real sister. Though she is ten years older than me, I feel I have a stronger connection with her because we have the same father. We have the same genetic makeup and some of the same traits as well. (Female with stepbrothers and stepsisters and one half sister)

When two or more full siblings are present, thirteen respondents (87 percent) choose one of their full siblings as their favorite sibling. Despite normative beliefs (treating family members the same regardless of genetic relatedness), either internalized or externally imposed by parents, respondents overwhelmingly identify a full sibling as their favorite sibling. Respondents are aware of genetic differences between them, their full siblings, their half siblings and their stepsiblings. Stepsiblings are often not considered to be part of the family possibly because they were not raised together. Thus residency and time do matter in this case. Table 3 provides an overview of which sibling is preferred as the favorite sibling.

Of the five respondents who did not want to identify a favorite sibling, four grew up with one full sibling and one or more half siblings. One of them was raised with six full siblings and four half siblings. Exposure to half siblings (e.g., co-residence) may make it more difficult to choose a favorite between full siblings and half siblings. If those five with no preference were not included in the distribution, the picture that emerges is even more telling: 31 out of 35 (89 percent) favor a full sibling over other siblings and four (11 percent) favor a half sibling over a full sibling.

Table 3.

Preference and Number of Full Siblings Present

Preference	One Full Sibling	Two or More FS	Total
FS over HS	10	7	17
FS over SS	4	6	10
FS over HS and SS	4	0	4
HS over FS	3	1	4
HS over SS	0	0	0
SS over FS	0	0	0
SS over HS	0	0	0
No Preference	4	1	5
Total	25	15	40

When people do have stepsiblings, they are not seen as a valuable commodity.

> I do have step siblings but I don't really consider them family. (Female 19-years of age - not living with her stepsiblings)

Other respondents voice concerns about the possibility of obtaining half siblings and stepsiblings or express happiness when stepsiblings are no longer present.

> I thankfully do not have any stepsiblings. I do have a stepmother but she is not able to conceive due to health problems. I could not be happier about that! (Female with one older brother)

> I do not have any step or half siblings and am very thankful for that. A lot of my friends have broken families and I see how that tears them apart. (Female in traditional nuclear family)

> I currently have no stepsiblings. When my dad remarried, my step-mom had twin daughters. I never liked them and never acknowledged them as family because there was something "off" with them. When my dad and step-mom separated I was relieved that I didn't have to pretend to like them anymore. I had nothing against either parent remarrying, or my dad having two stepdaughters. What bugged me was that they were rude and spoiled and had no respect for my sister or myself. (Female with one sister)

Yet for others, genetic makeup does not really matter and family members are treated equally.

> I don't really have a favorite sibling. I am an equal opportunity harasser. I am always fighting with them. I'm the one that's always bossing them around and at the same time they gang up on me whenever they can. They probably have each other as favorite sibling but as I said, I like to harass them equally if I can. (Male with an older brother and three half siblings whom he does not see often)

> I also have three step-brothers, who are like real brothers to me. (Female with one sister and three stepbrothers. She favors her full sister)

> I do not have a favorite sibling. However, I can say that I have a different bond with my real brother and sister than I do with any of my step siblings even though I have also known my step siblings all my life. (Female with two full siblings and three stepsiblings – two stepbrothers and one stepsister)

Some respondents express an eagerness to get to know each other better.

> Even though we live far apart and we rarely talk, I hope that later on in life when he gets older we can make up for lost times and have a better relationship. (Female writing about her half brother)

Respondents who do not have full siblings (N = 7) and respondents who do not indicate a favorite sibling (N = 5) were later omitted from the analysis. Thus 35 respondents in remarried families had some combination of full siblings, half siblings or stepsiblings in their family of orientation.

Conservative tests for significance are performed. The one sample Chi-square test is a nonparametric test. "Nonparametric tests are known as distribution-free tests because they make no assumptions about the underlying data. In general, the parametric versions of tests are more sensitive than the nonparametric versions and should be used when you reasonably believe that the necessary assumptions are met" (SPSS Base 10.0 Applications Guide 1997:231). The Chi-square test compares observed with expected values (Reynolds 1977). Preference for a full sibling (over half siblings and stepsiblings) is statistically significant (X^2 = 20.83, df 2, $p \leq .001$). If the seven respondents with no full sibling present, who by lack of choice indicated a half sibling, are included in the analysis, the results are still statistically significant (X^2 = 33.86, df 2, $p \leq .001$). Even, if the original 65 respondents in remarried families were included in the analysis (including singletons, full siblings only, half siblings only, stepsiblings only), the result would still be statistically significant (X^2 = 35.99, df 3, $p \leq .001$). Full siblings are preferred over half siblings and stepsiblings. The following statements reflect an emphasis on biology and may indicate that sharing the same mother is more powerful than sharing the same father. However, it may also be an indication that residency matters. The majority of children tend to reside with their mother after a divorce and during the remarriage of their mother.

> One thing that I'll always take with me the rest of my life is no matter the situation family always comes first. Blood is thicker than water. (Female in traditional nuclear family)

> The number one reason why he is my favorite sibling is that we have the same mother. (Female favoring her full brother over her half sister)

Does the number of full siblings effect the choice of type of favorite sibling (full, half or step)? Since the independent variable is measured on an interval level, a regression analysis is the appropriate test for significance. An ANOVA shows that there is an effect (F = 16.18, df 64, p ≤ .001). The number of full siblings present explains 20 percent of the variance in the type of favorite sibling. However, the effect is negative since the beta equals -.45. If more full siblings are present, then one is slightly inclined to choose a half sibling in order to avoid playing favorites among full siblings? The number of half siblings and the number of stepsiblings do not have an effect on choice of type of favorite sibling (F = 1.39, df 64, n.s., and F = .77, df 64, n.s. respectively).

Is the respondent's gender associated with the choice of sibling? Because these data are measured on a nominal level, the question is addressed with a Chi-square test (Crosstabs). The answer is no (X^2 =.14, df 3, n.s.). Gender does not matter. The next section describes relationships between full siblings.

Full Siblings

One hundred and ten respondents who submitted the assignment were raised in traditional nuclear families. The sample consisted of 38 percent males (N = 42) and 62 percent females (N = 68). Respondents' number of full siblings ranges from 0 to 6. Birth order positions for respondent are as follows: oldest child (41 percent), middle child (20 percent) and youngest child (39 percent). Birth order positions for favorite sibling are: oldest (31 percent), middle (18 percent) and youngest (38 percent). Twelve respondents (or 12 percent) did not want to choose a favorite sibling and two respondents did not indicate the birth order of their favorite sibling. Respondents who are the firstborn (N = 46) tend to have a preference for the youngest child (29 firstborns), and middle children (N = 21) tend to have a preference for the youngest child (9 middle children) and for another middle child. These preferences are statistically significant; thus there is an association between birth order of respondent and birth order of favorite sibling

($X^2 = 60.24$, df 6, $p \leq .001$). Both firstborns and middle-borns favor the youngest child. The favoritism is reciprocated for the oldest because the youngest siblings tend to prefer their oldest sibling.

The birth of a younger sibling can have a huge impact on respondents:

> It was a total shock, but I was so unbelievable happy to know I was going to have a little brother or sister to help take care of. (Female who writes about the news of getting a sibling when she was ten years old)

Or consider this view, as expressed by a 17-year old female who became sister to a baby brother at age four.

> I felt as if my world had crumbled down. Everyone would always pay more attention to him and never me, I thought, so I tried many times to 'accidentally' kill him. My mom said that I would lay on top of him or cover him up in as many blankets I could find.

Respondents in traditional nuclear families tend to have a preference for a sibling who is close in age. Eighty-two percent report that the age difference between them and their favorite sibling is five years or less. The remaining 18 percent have an age difference between six years and 16 years.

Respondents' gender is not a determining variable in the choice (oldest, middle, and youngest) of favorite sibling ($X^2 = 2.32$, df 3, n.s.). Neither is there a preference for a sibling who is of the same gender ($X^2 = 2.60$, df 2, n.s.).

Respondents in traditional nuclear families who did not grow up with siblings (N = 5) identify friends, cousins and even animals in sibling terms:

> I have had my animals for 14 years and they fill the void of being alone. (Female singleton)

The presence of pets is not always comforting as voiced by a female singleton:

> I am an only child that unfortunately has to share all the attention with the family dog.

Respondents who did not want to identify a favorite sibling (N = 12), articulated why by stating the following reasons:

> I don't have a favorite sibling; there is something special that I have with each of my siblings. (18-year old female with four siblings: a 24-year old brother, a 19-year old sister, a 16-year old sister and a 10-year old sister in a traditional nuclear family)

> I do not have a favorite sibling. I am really, really close with all of my siblings. (20-year old female with 1 sister and 2 brothers)

Siblings who do identify a favorite give a variety of reasons: citing that the sibling is their best friend, that they have the same preferences pertaining to movies, books and music, and that they are interested in the same sports (i.e., play basketball together). Sisters like to hang out with each other, and go shopping together. Oftentimes, respondents indicate that they get along better now that they are in their late teens than when they were younger. Eldest children generally do not want younger children tagging along when they are with their friends and invading their space when they are at home. However, with time comes appreciation and age differences seem to subside when children are in their teens. Both sexes voice their love for their sibling in similar ways:

> My sister is like my best friend and I would not trade her for the world. (Male)

> My brother is, in all actuality, my best friend. (18-year old female writing about her 23-year old brother)

> My favorite sibling is my brother, but this is not because he is my only sibling. I think he would be my favorite even if I had more brothers and sisters. (20-year old female)

Other people are more ambivalent about their sibling(s):

> We were never close like a lot of sisters are. Now that we are older we get along much better, of course it helps that we live in different states. (Female writing about her relationship with her only sibling who is three years older)

> I have only one sister, so at times she is my favorite sister and sometimes she is the most annoying person on this planet. (Female describing her two year younger sister)

Distance between siblings is not uncommon. There is a tendency to disengage from the family during early and middle adolescence (12-to-16-year olds), thus leading to an overall decrease in family cohesion (Baer 2002). Sibling relationships become less important when adolescents make a transition into adulthood and become more important later in life (White 2001).

Some respondents are less flattering about their sibling:

> I fortunately only have one sibling. (18-year old female about her brother)

> My sister just turned thirteen, so you can imagine what life is like under that roof. She screams all day long, complains all night long, and doesn't seem to have the slightest need for sleep. (19-year old male describing his sister)

> Growing up, most siblings bicker like there is no tomorrow, but for some odd reason, I can only recall arguing with Curtis once or twice. (Female about her five year older brother in a traditional nuclear family)

The presence of a full sibling can be experienced as a pleasure, someone to do stuff with, and can be experienced as a nuisance. The bickering and rivalry over parental attention when siblings are children seem a precondition for establishing close bonds in later childhood and adulthood. Fights are almost a necessary condition for bonding later in the life course. Further, full siblings cannot escape each other and need to resolve their differences because they are living in the same house.

Full Siblings and Half Siblings

In remarried families where half siblings and stepsiblings are present, if they do not live in the same house they are visitors and may at best be treated as visitors and they may be tolerated as guests or seen as intruders. In these cases the respondent is not forced to try to build a relationship with half and stepsiblings or to resolve issues that may arise between them since their stay is only temporary. The respondent can just wait it out because the problem will resolve itself with the return of the half sibling and/or stepsibling to their own residence.

We have seen that siblings like to bond with siblings close in age. Half siblings are likely to have a larger age gap with the respondent than possible full siblings. Parental adjustment to a divorce and meeting a new spouse takes time so half siblings may not be produced within the timeframe of preference: within five years. A greater age gap may be a possible explanation for the fact that in remarried families there is a preference for full siblings.

In the dataset for remarried families, the mean age difference between the respondent and his or her full sibling favorite is 3.23 years, between the respondent and the half sibling favorite is 10.79 years, and between the respondent and the stepsibling favorite is 7.5 years. These differences are statistically significant (F = 2.54, df 42, p ≤ .05).

Dummy variables are created, identifying whether the favorite sibling is a full sibling (value 1) or not (value 0), and whether the favorite sibling is a half sibling (value 1) or not (value 0). In addition dummy variables are created for age difference (equal or less than 5 years and more than 5 years).

When the age gap is less or equals five years, there is a preference for a full sibling since 88 percent of respondents indicate that their preferred sibling is a full sibling who is between five years older or younger than the respondent. (X^2 =

18.94, df 1, p ≤ .001). Apparently, closeness in age indeed fosters friendship bonds among siblings. When the favorite sibling is a half sibling, in 72 percent of cases, there is an age difference of six years and more. This result is significant (X^2= 22.18, df 1, p ≤ .001). Half siblings may be perceived as the new cute and adorable baby and may evoke motherly feelings in an older female sibling, and a sense of protection in an older brother, especially when older siblings are on good terms with their stepparent. Because it was not the scope of the research project there is no data available on relationships with stepparents. However, it is an interesting topic worth further investigation.

Favorite Sibling and Type of Solidarity

In the 'Family of Orientation' Assignment (question 4 B), respondents indicate why they identify a sibling as their favorite sibling. The question was an open-ended question and generated a variety of reasons why a particular sibling is the favorite. I clustered the answers according to the typology of solidarity discussed in chapter four (e.g., functional solidarity, associational solidarity, and affectual solidarity). Whenever people stated: 'we have fun together', 'like to hang out together', 'do stuff together', 'someone to play with', or 'fight a lot and laugh a lot', those reasons were coded as associational solidarity. When reasons included: 'because we are close in age', 'we have a small age gap', or 'we share a bond because we are close in age', or 'I feel close to him', those reasons were coded as affectual solidarity (emotional closeness). When reasons were: 'helps me with homework', 'helps me with problems', 'I want to protect her', 'gives me money', or 'sends presents', those reasons were an indication of functional solidarity and they were coded as such. Whenever respondents indicated they did not have a favorite or mentioned that they loved or disliked all their siblings equally their response was coded as no favorite sibling.

Nineteen respondents indicated they admired their favorite sibling for a variety of reasons such as working hard, having a pleasant personality, or being a good role model. The category miscellaneous consist of a mixed variety of reasons such as 'does not beat me up' (N = 2), 'because he is my only full sibling', and 'because we grew up together'. Table 4 presents the different types of solidarity.

Table 4.

Favorite Sibling and Type of Solidarity

Reasons	Frequency	Percentage	Traditional Family	Other Family
No Favorite Sibling	37	17 %	16	21
Associational Solidarity	71	33 %	50	21
Functional Solidarity	47	22 %	21	26
Affectual Solidarity	23	11 %	10	13
Admires Sibling	19	9 %	10	9
Miscellaneous	17	8 %	3	14
Total	214	100 %	110	104

Is there a difference in type of solidarity between respondents who grew up in a traditional nuclear family and respondents who were part of other types of families (e.g., remarried, widowed, divorced and single parent families)? As we have seen, 110 respondents are from traditional nuclear families and 105 respondents are from other types of families. A Chi-square test identifies that indeed there is a difference ($X^2 = 21.41$, df 6, $p \leq .005$). Respondents in traditional nuclear families report more associational solidarity as a reason why they identify a sibling as their favorite sibling compared to respondents who grew up in other types of families (N = 50 versus N = 21) and respondents in other types of families identify reasons in the miscellaneous category more than respondents in traditional nuclear families (N= 14 versus N = 3).

Associational solidarity is the main reason for respondents in traditional nuclear families in addressing why they choose a particular sibling. They like to hang out with the sibling, to have fun together, to share activities such as playing basketball and bike riding, and they indicate they like the same things as their favorite sibling. The main reason (just slightly more than associational solidarity) for respondents, who grew up in other family constellations, is functional solidarity. They give and /or receive support from the favorite sibling. They receive financial assistance and provide or get help with homework. The favorite sibling is also a source for helping with problems and giving advice. In other words, the favorite sibling is the person who is there for the respondent and helps in times of trouble. This phenomenon can be explained by the fact that respondents who grew up in other family constellations have generally experienced more trauma than respondents who grew up in a traditional nuclear family. Respondents in widowed, single parent, and divorced families had to cope with the death of a parent or a divorce so there is only one parent present in the household. In the case of a remarriage of their parent, they face the challenge of adjusting to their new family member(s). Their favorite sibling provides or receives instrumental support and assistance. The differences between type of family and reasons for choosing the favorite sibling are significant ($X^2 = 45.03$, df 30, $p \leq .05$). The following section examines the results from the secondary data sets: the 1986, 1994 and 2002 waves of the General Social Survey.

Findings from the 1994 General Social Survey

The 1994 General Social Survey provides information about family and the way respondents' siblings and respondents' children are related to the respondent. The 1994 wave of the General Social Survey succinctly provides information about some indicators pertaining to solidarity. The dataset provides rich data about family background variables, including family of orientation and family of procreation. I first describe the demographic variables and then turn to the analyses of sibling solidarity.

Of the 2,992 respondents, 43 percent (N = 1,290) were male and 57 percent (N = 1,702) were female. The mean age is 45.97 years (SD. 17.05). Respondents identified themselves as white (83 percent), black (13 percent) or other (4 percent). Respondents are Protestant (60 percent), Catholic (26 percent), or Jewish (2 percent). Four percent identifies another religion and eight percent of respondents are not religious.

The dataset includes 2,992 respondents who have 5,545 children. A total of 820 respondents do not have any children. The remaining respondents (N = 2,172) have 2.6 children (ranging from one child to eight or more). The 1994 General Social Survey provides data pertaining to genetic relationship of 2,966 children. The majority of children are respondents' biological offspring (nearly 93 percent).

Pertaining to marital status: 51.5 percent (N = 1,541) are currently married, 20.5 percent of the respondents (N = 614) have never married, 9.6 percent (N = 288) are widowed, and 18.3 percent are divorced or legally separated (N = 548). The category married includes respondents in first and higher order marriages.

A subset of respondents (N = 1,199) answered questions about their previous marital history. Twenty-six percent had been married before and 74 percent were not married before. When comparing whether the respondent had married before (yes/no) and their current spouse had married before (yes/no), it is revealed that most respondents who were married before, married a spouse who had also married before (66 percent) and respondents who were not married before were now married to a spouse who had also not married before (88 percent). Eleven percent of the respondents who were married before, had married a spouse who had never married before and 34 percent of the respondents who were not married before, had married a spouse who had previously been married (X^2 = 215.48, df 1, $p \leq .001$). These findings are in agreement with earlier reports by Ganong and Coleman (1994). Table 5 presents an overview of children and parent's relatedness.

Table 5.

Children and Parent's Relatedness

Child Number	Biological	Adopted	Step
1	1,043	21	59
2	831	13	36
3	445	6	31
4	224	4	17
5	107	1	10
6	48	1	9
7	30	0	5
8	14	1	1
9	8	1	0
Total	2,750 (92.7%)	48 (1.6 %)	168 (5.6%)

Respondents have a total of 11,064 siblings. The number of siblings ranges from 0 (N = 162) to 35. Five respondents indicated that they do not know how many siblings they have. Respondents were asked follow-up questions about a maximum of nine siblings pertaining to blood relationship and siblings' gender. The majority of siblings (85 percent) are full siblings. The sex of 10,008 siblings is known. Respondents report to have a total of 4,948 female siblings (49 percent) and a total of 5,060 male siblings (51 percent). Table 6 provides information about siblings and their genetic relatedness.

Table 6.

Number of Siblings and Genetic Relatedness

Type of Sibling	Number	Percentage
Full	8,501	85 %
Adopted	93	1 %
Step	452	5 %
Half	929	9 %
Total	9,975	100 %

Respondents with siblings (N = 2,662) were asked to pick one sibling for follow-up questions pertaining to the sibling's education and the sibling's work experience. The majority of respondents selected their first sibling (N = 1,136 or 43 percent), followed by the second sibling (N = 637 or 24 percent), the third sibling (N = 377 or 14 percent) and fourth sibling (N = 213 or 8 percent). The first sibling is the sibling who is closest in age followed by the second sibling, third sibling and so forth.

When the first sibling was selected, in 90 percent of cases it was a full sibling. Step and half siblings were chosen in 8 percent of cases. When the second sibling was selected, in 89 percent of cases it was a full sibling. Step and half siblings were picked in 9 percent of cases. When the third sibling was selected, in 85 percent of cases it was a full sibling. Half sibling and stepsibling were picked in 14 percent of cases. When the fourth sibling was chosen in 88 percent of cases it was a full sibling, and in 12 percent it was a half or a stepsibling. Adopted siblings are excluded from the following Table.

Table 7.

Sibling Picked and Genetic Relatedness

Sibling picked	Percentage	Full Sib	Half and Step Sib
First sibling	43 %	90 %	8 %
Second sibling	24 %	89 %	9 %
Third Sibling	14 %	85 %	14 %
Fourth Sibling	8 %	88 %	12 %
Total	89 %		

Thus, the sibling selected for follow-up questions is not only the sibling closest in age, but in most instances also a full sibling. We cannot conclude that this choice for a sibling is driven by genetic relatedness. We have seen earlier, as reported by college students, that closeness in age promotes friendship bonds among siblings. Full siblings usually grow up together thus residency may matter since there are more opportunities for interactions on a daily basis. Table 8 provides data about which sibling is chosen and what the genetic relatedness to the respondent is. The choice of the sibling when compared to the numbers and percentages of full siblings, half siblings and stepsiblings follows the siblings present.

Table 8.

Siblings and Relationship

Sib	Full Sib	Adopt	Half Sib	Step Sib	N	% FS	% HS	% SS	N.A.
1st Sib	2,441	40	209	91	2,781	88	8	3	171
2nd Sib	1,940	20	175	89	2,224	87	8	4	721
3rd Sib	1,401	12	162	73	1,648	85	12	4	1,297
4th Sib	956	5	124	66	1,151	83	11	6	1,794
5th to 9th Sib	1,763	16	259	133	2,171	81	12	6	12,636

A subset of the 1994 General Social Survey provides insights if respondents socialize with their sibling(s) and how frequently they socialize with their siblings. These data are provided in Table 9.

Table 9.

Socializing with Sibling

Spend Evening with Sib(s)	N	Percentage
No sibs	45	8.9 %
Almost daily	17	3.4 %
Several times a week	63	12.5 %
Several times a month	57	11.3 %
Once a month	54	10.7 %
Several times a year	110	21.8 %
Once a year	92	18.2 %
Never	67	13.3 %
Total	505	100 %

When respondents with no siblings are excluded from the analysis, the total number of respondents equals 460. For the purposes of comparison, I created three categories: frequent socializing (almost daily to once a month), infrequent socializing (once a year or several times a year) and socializes never.

Because the variable socialization with sibling(s) is phrased: 'Do you spend an evening with a sibling?', comparing a group which contains a mixture of full siblings and half siblings and/or stepsiblings with a group which has full siblings only would not represent the outcome in an adequate manner, as respondents may frequently socialize with their full sibling(s) but never with their stepsibling(s). Therefore, I created sibling groups that consist solely of full siblings and solely of half siblings and stepsiblings by using dummy variables (0 = blended group, 1 = full siblings only). Chi-square analyses are performed comparing groups of full siblings with groups of half and stepsiblings and the frequency of spending an evening with a sibling.

When the results of the Chi-squares are examined, it is obvious that when the sibling group consists of full siblings only there is more frequent socialization with a sibling than among siblings groups that consists of half and step siblings. In addition, the pattern is a higher incidence among blended sibling groups to never spend an evening with a sibling. However, the results are not statistically significant when the respondent has one sibling, two siblings, or three siblings, although there is a higher incidence among blended sibling groups (step and half siblings only) to never spend an evening with a sibling. No analyses are conducted with larger sibling groups, because of violations of statistical assumptions (e.g., too many empty cells). Based on the results, there is a pattern among respondents in larger blended sibling groups to have less contact with their half siblings and stepsiblings. Table 10 presents an overview of the Chi-square test results.

Table 10.

Number of Sibling(s), Type of Sibling and Frequency of Socialization

Number of Siblings	Chi-Square	df	P value	N
One Sib	1.95	2	P = 0.38	443
Two Sibs	3.23	2	P = 0.20	329
Three Sibs	3.75	2	P = 0.15	225
Four Sibs	6.54	2	P = 0.04**	134
Five Sibs	7.14	2	P = 0.03**	87
Six Sibs	6.67	2	P = 0.04**	68

** Significant at the .005 level

Does marital status influence socialization with one's siblings? Marital status does indeed matter. The respondents who have never been married, spend an evening with a sibling much more frequently than the married, divorced and widowed respondents (X^2 = 51.31, df 28, p ≤ .001). Twenty one percent of the never married spend evenings with a sibling several times a week. Since this effect may be attributed to age, I created three age categories: between 18 and 30, between 31 and 49, and 50 plus. The majority of the never married are between the ages of 18 and 30 (55 percent), and because of their younger age, they may still live at home with their parents and siblings, or live in the same town as their parents and their siblings. In the case of the 'never married' category, proximity would then account for the frequency of spending time with one's siblings (Chi-square for marital status and three age groups: X^2 = 969.69, df 8, $p \leq .001$). However, only four percent of respondents aged 30 and less, report to spend an evening with a sibling on a daily basis and 24 percent report to spend an evening with a sibling several times per week which is significantly more than those respondents who are older (Chi-square for three age categories and socialization with sibling: X^2 = 59.14, df 14, $p \leq .001$). Nevertheless, twenty three percent of married respondents spend an evening with a sibling several times per year.

When this variable is recoded and collapsed in fewer categories, an obvious pattern emerges: married respondents report spending an evening with their sibling(s) more frequent compared to the widowed and separated (41 percent, 26 percent and 28 percent respectively). It is remarkable that the widowed and divorced respondents are over-represented in the category that lists that they never spend an evening with a sibling (26 percent of widowed and 19 percent of divorced respondents). A statistical analysis shows: X^2 = 18.49, df 8, $p \leq .05$. This result is in contrast to assumptions by scholars such as Rosenberg and Anspach (1973) who believe that after marital dissolution (whether through divorce or death of a spouse), siblings will become more important. Divorced and widowed people should supposedly reconnect with their siblings. In this particular instance it is not the case.

How do age and marital status effect spending an evening with a sibling?
In a regression analysis with age and marital status as independent variables and spending an evening with a sibling as the dependent variable, only age showed an

effect: six percent of the variance can be attributed to age (F= 13,64, df 2, p ≤ .001). Younger respondents (between the ages of 18 and 30) tend to spend more evenings with a sibling than their older counterparts.

Is there a difference between frequency of interaction with siblings and frequency of interaction with parents? There emerges a consistent pattern that is statistical significant (X^2 = 417.61, df 49, p ≤.001). Respondents who tend to spend an evening with a parent several times per week also spend an evening with a sibling several times per week. The same pattern holds true for spending an evening with parents several times per year and spending an evening with a sibling several times per year. It is likely that spending an evening with parent(s) and sibling(s) occurs simultaneously while celebrating holidays and/or birthdays with the entire family of orientation. Those respondents who never spend an evening with siblings tend to also never spend an evening with parent(s).

Is there a difference between the married and unmarried on the dimension of frequency of interaction with parents? The never married spend an evening with their parents more frequently compared to the married, widowed and divorced respondents. Twenty-six percent of the never married spend an evening with a parent several times per week. The differences are even more pronounced for respondents who report to never spend an evening with a parent. The widowed and divorced are overrepresented in this category (24 percent of the widowed and 22 percent of divorced respondents), followed by the separated (20 percent), married (15 percent of married respondents never spend and evening with their parent), and the never married respondents (3 percent). These differences are significant (X^2 = 129.02, df 28, p ≤ .001). The total number of cases in this subset is 503.

When respondents who report that they do not have (living) parents are excluded from the Chi-square analysis (N = 377), the difference between the groups becomes even more powerful. For example, 75 percent of the widowed people in the sample, and 27 percent of the divorced people in the sample, report that they never spend an evening with a parent ($X^2 = 61.64$, df 12, $p \leq .001$).

Pertaining to spending an evening with a parent, is there a difference among sibling groups that contain full siblings only and sibling groups that consist of half and stepsiblings? Regression analyses show no significant effect. However, when a respondent has four full siblings, there is a significant effect that is negative (F = 6.62, df 134, $p \leq .01$) Thus siblings in blended sibling groups with four step or half siblings spend an evening with their parents more frequently than siblings who are each other's full siblings. There is a pattern that when the sibling group consists of half siblings and stepsiblings they tend to socialize more often (e.g., spending an evening) with a parent.

Findings from the 1986 and 2002 General Social Survey

Demographic variables from respondents in the 1986, 1994 and 2002 General Social Survey are comparable as can be seen in Table 11.

Table 11.

Background Variables GSS years 1986, 1994, and 2002

Variables	1986	1994	2002
Mean Age	45.43	45.97	46.28
SD. Age	17.80	17.05	17.37
N	1463	2986	2751
Male	42.2 %	43.1%	44.4 %
Female	57.8 %	56.9 %	55.6 %

In 1986 and 2002, several indicators for functional solidarity, associational solidarity and affectual solidarity are included in the General Social Survey. Respondents answered questions about whom they would ask for a loan, whom they would turn to for help when they were sick, and whom they would ask for help with household chores. These are indicators of instrumental help and assistance and thus correspond with functional solidarity. Table 12 provides insights into which person is asked for which type of functional solidarity.

Table 12.

Functional Solidarity in Percentages

Year	Functional Solidarity	Spouse	Sibling	Parent	Child	Friend	Other	N
1986	Borrow1	14	7	20	6	4	49	1,401
1986	Borrow2	2	12	17	8	12	49	1,382
2002	Borrow1A	13	11	31	6	5	34	1,130
2002	Borrow2A	4	14	22	6	9	45	1,130
1986	Sick1	52	6	11	13	10	8	1,408
1986	Sick2	4	12	14	23	21	26	1,396
2002	Sick1A	48	7	14	12	10	9	1,142
2002	Sick2A	7	11	19	23	16	24	1,133
1986	Chores1	50	7	6	15	10	12	1,409
1986	Chores2	4	10	10	24	21	31	1,399

In 1986, when large sums of money are needed, the majority of respondents (39 percent) contact their bank for a loan (in category 'other'). In 2002, only 8 percent go to the bank for a loan. In 1986, the bank was the first choice of respondents, regardless of marital status, except for the never married for whom the first and second choice to borrow money from are father (25 percent) and mother (21 percent) respectively before going to the bank (21 percent). The differences are significant ($X^2 = 455.24$, df 60, $p \leq .001$). In 2002, for the majority of respondents, the bank was not the first choice for borrowing a large sum of money. For married people their spouse is their first choice (21 percent of married people), for the never married their mother (26 percent) and father (24 percent) are preferred, while the widowed prefer to borrow money from a daughter (17 percent) or son (16 percent) first before seeking other options ($X^2 = 96.75$, df 64, p $\leq$ .001). Parents, spouses and the respondents' children are generally preferred over siblings in providing instrumental help and assistance, although siblings are asked for help by approximately 10 percent of respondents. Functional solidarity seems more intergenerational (i.e., parents and children) in nature than intra-generational (i.e., siblings).

Affectual solidarity (or feelings of emotional closeness) is represented by questions about whom respondents turn to for help when they are upset, when they are depressed and when they face major life changes. Variables upset 1 and upset 2 reflect to whom respondent turns to first and second for help with marital problems. Variables down 1 and down 2 measure to whom the respondent turns to first and second for help when depressed. It is clear that a close friend is overwhelmingly preferred as the first person to turn to for help with marital problems. When one is depressed, the spouse is the first person most respondents turn to for help. Affectual solidarity and its indicators are presented in Table 13.

It is obvious that close friends play a more important role than siblings. However, there is a difference that is based on marital status. The never married, divorced and separated respondents prefer to talk to their closest friend when they are upset (43 percent, 38 percent and 37 percent respectively). Only 21 percent of married people prefer to talk to their closest friend ($X^2 = 276.41$, df 64, p $\leq$ .001).

Table 13.

Affectual Solidarity in Percentages

Year	Affectual Solidarity	Spouse	Sibling	Parent	Child	Friend	Other	N
1986	Upset1	7	11	15	10	29	28	1,397
1986	Upset2	1	12	11	8	26	42	1,417
1986	Down1	40	8	6	7	27	12	1,378
1986	Down2	6	12	12	11	36	23	1,403
2002	Down1A	32	9	11	6	31	11	1,139
2002	Down2A	11	15	16	11	25	22	1,137
1986	Change1	49	6	13	10	11	11	1,413
1986	Change2	3	12	23	16	23	23	1,390

The divorced, separated, and never married respondents are slightly more inclined to turn to their sisters for support when they are upset than the married respondents (9, 10 and 12 percent versus 7 percent respectively). The widowed respondents prefer their daughter (20 percent) and son (11 percent).

When respondents are depressed the first person they talk to, in the case of married respondents, is the spouse (63 percent), for the never married it is their closest friend (45 percent) and the same holds true for the widowed, divorced and separated (28 percent, 43 percent and 37 percent respectively). The differences are significant ($X^2 = 662.05$, df 64, $p \leq .001$). In addition, the unmarried turn to their sister more than the married. The same pattern still holds true in 2002, although daughter and sister are listed as second and third person to turn to for the widowed respondents ($X^2 = 488.25$, df 64, $p \leq .001$).

The next section discusses associational solidarity. Associational solidarity is measured by questions about the frequency of contact with siblings. How often does the respondent visit with a sister and/or brother and how often does the respondent call the sister or brother? Table 14 depicts several indicators of associational solidarity.

Table 14.
Associational Solidarity in Percentages

Indicators	Frequent	Infrequent	Hardly ever	Year	N
Visit sister	52	22	26	1986	1,047
Contact sister	67	18	15	1986	1,018
Visit brother	47	25	28	1986	1,033
Contact brother	55	23	22	1986	997
Visit sib	56	24	20	2002	951
Contact sib	76	15	9	2002	925
Visit relative	68	20	12	1986	1,329
Contact relative	72	15	13	1986	1,290

Frequent contact and visits are defined as once a month or more. Infrequent contact equates several times per year. In 2002, a majority of respondents had frequently called or otherwise contacted a sibling (76 percent) while in 1986, only 55 percent had frequent contact with a brother and 67 percent had frequent contact with a sister. Respondent's gender influences the frequency of visiting one's sister: females tend to visit their sister more often than males (X^2 = 20.94, df 6, p $\leq$ .001). Travel time (proximity) to a sister explains 57 percent of the variance in visits to a sister (F = 1315.12, df 1015, p $\leq$ .001). Respondents who live in the proximity of their sister (half an hour or less), visit their sister more frequently than respondents who live farther away (X^2 = 954.67, df 35, p ≤ .001). The same pattern emerges for visits with a brother because 53 percent of the variance in visits is explained by travel time (F= 1131.06, df 991, p ≤ .001). Respondents who live in close proximity of their brother visit their brother more frequently than respondents who live more than a half hour drive away (X^2 =954.67, df 35, p ≤ .001). It is clear that associational solidarity among siblings is not declining as some family scholars suggest. Their argument is based on the fact that divorce and remarriage lead to a weakening of kinship ties. In this sample, which consists of married, never married, divorced, widowed and separated respondents, I found no evidence for this assumption. In this particular case, the 2002 General Social Survey showed more associational solidarity among siblings than the 1986 General Social Survey.

When asked which relative the respondent has the most contact with, mother-in-law tops the list with 15 percent, followed by sister-in-law (14 percent) and female relative (13 percent). Not surprisingly, marital status influences the choice of relative (X^2 = 596.44, df 48, p ≤ .001). Married respondents have a preference for their mother-in-law (25 percent of married respondents), widowed respondents have a preference for a granddaughter (21 percent) and another female relative (21 percent), while both divorced and separated respondents have a preference for an aunt (15 and 19 percent respectively) and another female relative (21 and 19 percent respectively). A female relative can be a sister, niece or cousin because they are lumped together in this category. The never married have a preference for a grandmother and an aunt (21 and 17 percent respectively).

The married respondents visit their brother and sister (1986 GSS) or sibling (2002 GSS) less frequent than the never married. This corresponds with Talcott Parsons' (1943) notion that siblings become less important when individuals start their own family of procreation. Marital status is a predictor of visiting/ calling brother, sister, or sibling in general. Further, there is more frequent contact with a sister than with a brother.

Limitations

By using a triangulation of methods, this study generated rich data. Participants in a series of "Blended Family Workshops' offered a valuable perspective on newly formed remarried families and the challenges they face.

Since most of the questions in the 'Family of Orientation' Assignment were open ended and college freshmen elaborated on their family, it contributed substantially in generating knowledge about remarried families and other types of family constellations. However, I compared data from first year college students (who tend to be between the ages of 17 and 22) with data obtained from the General Social Survey in which older adults were also included, thus leading to a higher mean age (45 years).

The college students, who have dealt with the divorce and/or remarriage of their parents, are reflecting upon a situation that is possibly still fresh in their mind. Therefore, residual effects of these traumatic events may still be present and linger on. The General Social Survey data are usually about adults later in the life course when people have started their own family of procreation or have had the ability to do so. It is plausible that when they themselves as adults have experienced divorce and remarriage that they will tend to be more understanding and compassionate about a divorce and remarriage in their family of orientation since they have become aware of the ramifications, whether emotionally or financially. In addition, adult children may not be as accurate in their recall, and may have a distorted, romanticized image of their childhood years or portray an exaggerated negative image of their traumatized childhoods. For example, Victoria Bedford (1998) found a positive reappraisal of childhood troubles in middle aged and older respondents.

By focusing on one respondent, both in the 'Family of Orientation' Assignment and within the General Social Survey data set, a researcher only obtains data on that particular person's beliefs and behavior and not about the entire sibling group. Further, using any data set generates limitations because the dataset is not developed to address a researcher's particular hypotheses. Questions in the 1994 General Social Survey were about one particular sibling and did not address the entire sibling group pertaining to indicators of solidarity. While the 1986 and 2002 General Social Survey generated data regarding solidarity, it did not offer a distinction as to genetic relatedness. While the 1994 General Social Survey included genetic relatedness, 85 percent of siblings are respondents' full siblings and about 93 percent of children are respondents' biological offspring.

However, by using several methods, I did obtain relevant data to assess the amount of solidarity among full siblings, half siblings and stepsiblings. I conclude that a continuation of sibling ties in adulthood remain important for people in contemporary American society. Moreover, adult siblings continue to assist each other when needed.

CHAPTER SIX
Conclusion and Discussion

This chapter first addresses the most important results of the research project and integrates the data obtained from the 'Blended Family Workshops', the 'Family of Orientation' Assignment, and the 1986, 1994 and 2002 General Social Survey. Then, the research hypotheses and their support or rejection are discussed. Lastly, overall conclusions are drawn and suggestions for future research are made.

Findings

College students indicate that they prefer a full sibling as their favorite sibling. The preference for the type of sibling is not affected by gender. When there is no full sibling available, the pattern is a preference for a half sibling (if present) followed by a stepsibling. Some respondents indicate they selected their full sibling as their favorite sibling because they had the same parents in common and were more of their own 'blood'. Whether this preference for a full sibling is driven by evolutionary theory principles or by cultural beliefs, such as a belief in the importance of blood relatives, is difficult to determine.

Interestingly, twenty percent of the variance in the choice of favorite sibling (full, half or step) is explained by the number of full siblings present, and this effect is negative. Whenever respondents have more full siblings, the half sibling or stepsibling becomes the favorite. It could be that attachment to one's sibling is diluted by the numbers of siblings or perhaps this phenomenon is an indication of not wanting to make a forced choice among full siblings, and, as a consequence, the default favorite sibling is the half sibling or stepsibling. Conversely, an older half sibling from their mother's or their father's previous marriage can serve as a role model and/or confidante and thus explain why a half sibling is favored. Since often the youngest sibling is the favorite it is possible that the baby of the family elicits protective and maternal/paternal feelings from the older sibling. It is likely that the baby is a product of the mother's remarriage, and thus technically a half sibling. Because Anderson (1999) found an increase in rivalry among full siblings in stepfamilies and less rivalry among half siblings and among stepsiblings, the choice of a half sibling or stepsibling as the favorite could be based on lower perceived rivalry. I encourage future research to determine if the effects of a larger group of full siblings are as substantial and persistent.

Respondents' birth order also influences their choice. Firstborns prefer the youngest sibling. That choice is mutual since respondents who are the lastborn often choose the oldest sibling as their favorite. Given the age difference between the oldest and youngest sibling, it is likely to presume that those siblings are each other's half siblings because it takes time after a divorce to remarry and it takes time to produce another child. When respondents choose a full sibling as their favorite, the mean age difference between them is three years; for respondents who choose their half sibling, the mean age difference is nearly 11 years; for respondent and favorite stepsibling there is about a 7 year age difference. Given that the majority of college students in the sample prefer a full sibling, it is also a sibling close in age. This preference for a sibling close in age could explain why the sibling of choice happens to be a full sibling since the age gap between full siblings is usually smaller than the age gap between half siblings and stepsiblings.

The effect of age is consistent with the literature (e.g., Stocker and McHale 1992). Stocker and McHale (1992) found that siblings close in age frequently fight but also display high levels of warmth toward each other. Being raised with a sibling close in age means the availability of a playmate while growing up with whom one can play, argue, and fight. Perhaps fighting and conflict (in the context of warmth) are prerequisites for developing affective bonds and emotional closeness that persist throughout one's life span.

When respondents were asked why they chose a particular sibling as a favorite sibling, there was a significant difference between respondents who grew up in a traditional nuclear family and respondents who were raised in another type of family constellation (i.e., remarried, divorced, widowed or single parent family). Reasons pertaining to associational solidarity were cited significantly more often by respondents from traditional nuclear families than by respondents from other types of families. For the latter, reasons associated with functional solidarity were the main source of identifying their favorite sibling. This sibling provides or receives instrumental help and assistance (such as protection, care taking and financial assistance), which in turn can bring about feelings of closeness among siblings who experience a traumatic event, such as a parent's death or their parents' divorce. Weaver, Ganong and Coleman (2003) make the same suggestion: "When resources normally sought from parents may not be available due to divorce or death, these may instead be received from sisters and brothers through provision of direct services" (p. 259). Recently, Voorpostel and Blieszner (2008) found a compensating mechanism among siblings; a poor relationship with their parent(s) enhances emotional support among brothers and sisters. Ihinger-Tallman notes: "In an environment that necessitates siblings meeting each other's needs when parents fail to meet them, siblings will increase their dependency upon one another, and consequently will be more tightly bonded" (1987b:171). When this notion holds true, there should be more functional solidarity between full siblings, half siblings, and stepsiblings in both divorced families and in remarried families compared to siblings in traditional nuclear families.

In deciding which sibling to name as their favorite, respondents from remarried families gave indeed more weight to the instrumental help and assistance they received from siblings (functional solidarity) than to the frequency of their interaction with siblings (associational solidarity). This finding differs from the finding in traditional nuclear families.

Married respondents in higher order marriages who participated in the 1994 General Social Survey, in the majority of cases (66 percent) were married to someone who also had been married before, which increases the likelihood of their parenting one or more stepchildren. This finding is consistent with the scholarly literature. Buckle, Gallup and Rodd (1996) found that divorced males with children are likely to remarry previously divorced women whereas divorced males without children tend to remarry females who had never been married. "...males with children from a previous marriage are making remarriage choices with caretaker provisions in mind, while those without children are making choices which place a premium on the prospective spouse's reproductive potential" (p. 376). Thus, the economic function of remarriage (obtaining a spouse to help raise children), as described by Elman and London (2001), is still important.

When asked to select a sibling for follow-up questions, respondents tend to choose the sibling closest in age who is also the respondent's full sibling. This pattern follows the siblings present in the family of orientation because the majority of siblings who are close in age are also the respondents' full siblings (in 90 percent of cases). Thus, it is difficult to distinguish whether similarity in age, proximity, parenting, or genetic relatedness influences this choice.

In answering the question 'How often do you spend an evening with a sibling?', 45 percent of respondents indicate they do this frequently (a range between almost daily to once a month). The never married respondents frequently spend an evening with a sibling, especially those between the ages of 18 and 30. This result corresponds with Parsons' (1943) notion that sibling ties in the family of orientation are important but are pushed into the second tier when a person marries and forms his or her own family of procreation.

What is remarkable is that married respondents socialize with a sibling more frequently than widowed and separated respondents. It would have been expected that the latter socialize more, given the fact that they do not have a spouse, and may turn to a sibling for support. My finding is contrary to earlier findings from Connides and Campbell (1995) who noticed closer ties among widowed-single sibling pairs and divorced-single sibling pairs as compared to married sibling pairs, and findings from White and Riedmann (1992a) who noticed that siblings are less important for the married. However, in my particular study, the wording of the question may have generated a potentially false conclusion. Respondents were asked about spending an *evening* with a sibling. It is possible that the widowed and divorced spend a lot of time with a particular sibling during weekdays and weekend days, just not evenings. It is also possible that the widowed and separated turn to their children or friends instead of their siblings and that sibling ties and parental ties are weakened once one moves from a family of orientation to a family of procreation, as is suggested by Parsons (1943). Recently, Sarkisian and Gerstel (2008) found that married men and women have indeed less intense intergenerational ties than the never married and divorced. Future research might prove fruitful in investigating the association between marital status and generational ties (i.e., contact with siblings).

In larger sibling groups (four or more siblings), there exists a pattern that respondents in sibling groups comprised of half siblings and stepsiblings, never spend an evening with a sibling. This pattern does not occur in smaller sibling groups. Anderson (1999) assumes that stepsibling relationships will be characterized by more distance. In my study, Anderson's assumption holds true for larger blended sibling groups but not for smaller groups. The 'dilution hypothesis', indicating that parents who have more children have less time and money for each individual child, may very well be applicable to larger sibling groups where each child must divide his attention among a great number of siblings, resulting in less cohesive sibling groups of siblings who grow up together but never really bond with one another.

The question becomes: Is there indeed less cohesion in larger sibling groups? Connides and Campbell (1995) found the opposite to be true because in their research, the number of siblings is positively related to closeness with siblings. "...larger families, appear to afford a greater opportunity for forming a sibling relationship marked by special closeness, extensive confiding, and high levels of contact" (p. 742). White (2001) also found that with a larger sibship there is greater affection, contact and support among siblings. Sibling contact should increase after a divorce of their parents. Perhaps their findings hold true for full sibling groups, but not for blended sibling groups. Spitze and Logan (1991) note that the more children parents have, the less attention and assistance they receive from each individual child in old age. The authors assume that both the adult children and their parents adjust their expectations of instrumental assistance in relation to the structure of the sibling group. However, larger blended sibling groups, consisting of four half and/or stepsiblings have a higher incidence of frequently spending an evening with a parent. When the blended sibling group is large, spending an evening with a sibling reportedly occurs infrequently, or never, while spending an evening with a parent occurs frequently. Thus, the number of siblings in blended sibling groups does affect cohesion among siblings but not cohesion with parents.

It is noteworthy to mention that, in general, respondents who socialize frequently with a sibling also frequently spend an evening with a parent and the same pattern holds true for respondents who report they infrequently socialize with a sibling. Those respondents, who report that they never spend an evening with a sibling, also never spend an evening with a parent. Horizontal socializing (siblings) is thus associated with intergenerational socializing (parents). Married respondents frequently spend an evening with a parent whereas 75 percent of widowed respondents and 27 percent of divorced respondents never spend an evening with a parent. It is plausible that spending an evening with a parent coincides with spending an evening with a sibling. The sibling(s) may be present during holidays or other family celebrations and spending an evening with a sibling is thus a byproduct of spending an evening with a parent.

When comparing the results of the 1986 and 2002 General Social Surveys, it is apparent that regarding functional solidarity, family has increasingly become important. Respondents turn to family (parents, spouse, and siblings) more often in 2002 than in 1986 as a source to borrow money. Siblings are asked for money in 11 percent of cases and they are asked as a first choice (preferred over a financial institution). I suspect that lending money to a sibling is more of an investment than offering advice or helping with an errand. Sibling ties are still meaningful in that siblings are there for one another when a brother or sister needs help. In providing help, Eriksen and Gerstel compare siblings to friends and note "... sibling and friends are relatively balanced "competitors" when it comes to the amount of help they receive" (2002:845). These scholars further conclude that family context matters. "Having a living parent facilitates caregiving among siblings, whereas greater family size forces adults to act judiciously about what and to whom they give" (p. 836). Further, as noted by Voorpostel and Van Der Lippe in a study based on a Dutch national sample, there is a preference for exchanging support with kin. "... people were more likely to exchange practical support with a sibling than with a friend" (2007:1276).

Respondents also quickly identify a parent as a source for help with financial problems. Apparently, there are ongoing obligations for parents to help their children. This result is not confined to the United States. Based on a study in The Netherlands, Van Gaalen and Dykstra (2006) found that adult "children are less likely to give financial support to their parents than to receive it from them" (p. 952). Coleman, Ganong and Cable (1997) found that family members feel obliged to help other family members in times of need. However, the obligation of the older generation to help their adult children is greater than the obligation of the children to help their elderly parents. These authors further found a stronger obligation among genetic kin than affinal kin (i.e., in-laws). Salmon and Daly note, "Contemporary North Americans, like other people, continue to rely on relatives, feeling both some entitlement to ask kin for help and some expectation that it will be willingly provided" (1996:293).

However, definitions of kinship have become more fluid. People cluster their family obligations in a hierarchy: first are self and children, then parents, then stepparents, then in-laws. People feel an obligation to help kin. Step kin, however, have to earn that help (Coleman and Ganong 2000).

Siblings also play a role in providing affectual solidarity, albeit a small one. When respondents experience marital problems, they overwhelmingly turn to a close friend, followed by a parent and a sibling. When respondents are depressed the tendency is to turn to a spouse first, although respondents also prefer a close friend or a sibling. Hoyt and Babchuck (1983) note that adults prefer members of their family of procreation as confidantes, especially spouses. Siblings do have a role in providing functional solidarity and affectual solidarity; however, they are most important in providing associational solidarity.

In comparing the results from both the 1986 General Social Survey and the 2002 General Social Survey pertaining to associational solidarity we cannot conclude a weakening of kinship ties among siblings, rather, the opposite holds true because 76 percent of respondents in 2002 have frequent contact with a sibling, and nearly 60 percent frequently visit a sibling, which is a little more than the 1986 General Social Survey findings. I found a gender difference which is in agreement with earlier research; both men and women have more frequent contact with a sister rather than with a brother (e.g., Connides and Campbell 1995; Eriksen and Gerstel 2002; Pulakos 1990; Salmon and Daly 1996; Weaver, Coleman and Ganong 2003).

The occurrence of more associational solidarity in 2002 than in 1986 does not necessarily mean that there are strong kinship ties in remarried families. The only conclusion that we can draw is that there is an increase in associational sibling solidarity that coexists with the fact that more and more families became remarried families between 1986 and 2002. Given the type of data, which does not provide information about genetic relatedness and includes information about just one or two particular siblings (to the exclusion of other siblings), I speculate that there is a more intense relationship with a full sibling when growing up in a household that also contains stepsibling(s) and half sibling(s) and that this full sibling is the focal sibling in addressing the General Social Survey questions. One common critique pertaining to studies about adult sibling ties is the overuse of two methodological strategies: the focus on the point of view of a single adult respondent or the focus on one selected sibling (Eriksen and Gerstel 2002).

Nevertheless, the triangulation of methods in the form of the 'Blended Family Workshop', the 'Family of Orientation' assignment, and the analyses of the 1986, 1994 and 2002 General Social Survey proved useful in examining family ties. The next section addresses my findings in relation to the specific research questions.

Hypotheses

The assumption that there is more functional solidarity among full siblings than among half siblings and stepsiblings (hypothesis 1A) is not supported. The opposite is the case since I found substantially more functional solidarity among respondents in families that have blended sibling groups. A possible explanation is that children who experience trauma such as a death or a divorce turn to their sibling(s) for instrumental help and assistance.

I expected to find more associational solidarity between full siblings than between half and stepsiblings (hypothesis 1B). This assumption is supported. Associational solidarity is cited as a reason for identifying a full sibling as their favorite sibling significantly more often than respondents who reported a half sibling or stepsibling was their favorite. In larger blended sibling groups there is less association with a sibling than in sibling groups that consist of full siblings only (General Social Survey 1994, variable: spend an evening with a sibling).

I expected to find more affectual solidarity between full siblings than between half and stepsiblings (hypothesis 1 C). In identifying a sibling as a favorite sibling, respondents from traditional nuclear families did not cite reasons pertaining to affectual solidarity more often than respondents from remarried families. Thus, there is no difference in the amount of affectual solidarity among full siblings, half siblings and stepsiblings.

It was predicted that same-sex siblings who are close in age would display more solidarity, regardless of genetic relatedness. This hypothesis was partly confirmed. Closeness in age promotes solidarity among siblings. Gender does not influence the choice of a favorite sibling. However, there is more frequent contact among sisters than among brothers. Scholars had already noted this distinction and suggest that women serve as kin keepers (e.g., Connides and Campbell 1995; Lee, Mancini and Maxwell 1990; Rosenthal 1985; Salmon and Daly 1996; Schmeeckle 2007).

Proximity influences the frequency with which respondents visit their brother or sister. Respondents who live close to their sibling (less than 30 minutes driving time) tend to visit that sibling more often than respondents whose sibling lives further away. Leigh (1982) had already noted a negative effect of geographical distance on contact with kin. Duberman (1973), based on a small sample (45 families) of dyadic relationships, concluded that stepsiblings who live in the same household have better relationships with each other than stepsiblings who live in separate households. Cross-sex stepsiblings particularly tend to have better relationships with each other than same-sex stepsiblings.

My findings indicate that there is slightly more overall solidarity between full siblings than among half siblings and stepsiblings. Unlike the findings from the 'Family of Orientation' study, the General Social Survey findings did not indicate that awareness of genetic relatedness is a discriminative factor in the overall solidarity among full siblings, half siblings and stepsiblings. There is an effect regarding the size of the sibling group. When there is a small group (less or equal to three siblings), there is no difference between sibling groups (blended siblings versus full siblings). When the group is larger, I found the following remarkable effect: blended siblings are much more likely to never spend an evening with a sibling while spending more time with their parents. Respondents in large blended sibling groups spend an evening with a parent more frequently than their full sibling counterparts in large sibling groups do.

Finally, it was assumed that married siblings, along Parsons' reasoning, would spend less time with a sibling than all other respondents. This hypothesis was partly confirmed. Married respondents did spend less time with a sibling than their single counterparts, especially when those singles are younger (between 18 and 30 years of age). However, married respondents spend more time with a sibling than divorced, widowed and separated respondents. It would be expected that the latter, given their marital status, would turn to their siblings for support. Instead, their friends and children fill that void.

Conclusion and Implications

Based on my research, I refute the notion that sibling ties have become solely symbolic in nature. Siblings, that is, full siblings, half siblings and stepsiblings, do have meaningful relationships with one another and I would argue that siblings still serve, as so eloquently outlined by Cumming and Schneider (1961), as a fundamental axis for emotional interaction. Moreover, family in general has become an important source of instrumental help and assistance as we have seen in the 2002 General Social Survey analysis pertaining to functional solidarity. The analysis of associational solidarity of the same year General Social Survey shows that siblings are still important persons in people's lives. They frequently visit with one another.

When I read the testimonies about the impact of divorce and remarriage on children, as articulated by college students, I could not detach myself emotionally from the subject matter at hand immediately. Of course children are scarred when their parents divorce. But they are also resilient and form close bonds with their full siblings and sometimes with their half siblings and stepsiblings. The point is that divorce and remarriage do not have a negative impact on children for life. Although these events may be initially upsetting, children are able to adjust to the divorce of their parents, and they are able to adjust again when their parents remarry. Siblings in blended families function and they function well. However, full sibling bonds are stronger than half sibling bonds unless half siblings are close in age (a maximum age difference of five years).

Remarried family life definitely has its challenges, especially in the first few years when every family member has to adjust to the new family. Ambivalence about one's position in the family (structural ambivalence), conflicting feelings about other family members (psychological ambivalence) and setting boundaries are important concepts during the first years of family formation as we have seen in statements from adults who participated in the 'Blended Family Workshops'. Further, the issue of boundaries in remarried families, or the lack thereof, was brought up by college students who were reared in this type of family.

Overall, remarried families are beneficial for children as is articulated in so many positive statements of college students who were raised in a blended type of family. Being part of a remarried family does not seem to affect their ability to develop close bonds later in life, although some of my students yearned for the traditional nuclear family or depicted their family as a romanticized picture of the nuclear family. Children who grew up in remarried families encountered problems but were able to establish close relationships with their siblings, whether they are full siblings, half siblings or step siblings. Parents in remarried families with younger stepchildren, can foster the bonds among their non-residential stepchildren, by providing opportunities for these children to 'hang out' together and thus providing a setting where these children can get to know each other better, possibly in cooperation with the former spouse.

The scholarly literature is adamant when it proclaims that children from divorced and remarried families are more prone to abuse from a stepfather or live-in boyfriend and are more likely to have teenage or out-of-wedlock pregnancies, to drop out of high school, to engage in criminal activities and to abuse drugs than children who are reared in traditional nuclear families. The statistics speak for themselves. However, when remarried families consist of loving (step)parents who are capable of setting and maintaining boundaries, who do not play favorites and who put the family first, those remarried families provide children with a loving and nurturing family environment that may possibly shield them from negative effects that other remarried families encounter. As observed by Cutrona (2004), commitment to a spouse is not permanent whereas the commitment to a child is permanent. Therefore, after a divorce, it is wise to be careful in selecting a new partner. In documenting subjective reasons for divorce, Amato and Previti (2003) obtained the following ranking: infidelity, incompatibility, drug use and growing apart. With these reasons in mind, people would be wise not to jump into a remarriage, but to go slowly and put their children's needs first. One of those needs is to have a father, even if he has a nonresidential status. Fagan and Barnett (2003) found that mothers play an instrumental role in fathers' involvement. They are gatekeepers who determine the amount of access a father has to his children. Anger and lack of paternal financial contributions negatively influence visitation issues. In addition, divorced fathers may legally end their child support obligations when their child turns eighteen (Wallerstein and Blakeslee [1989] 1990). This may affect their child's decision not to pursue a college degree. However, when the biological father has little or no contact with his child, "... a stepfather will tend to have more leeway asserting a paternal claim..." (Marsiglio 2004:30).

Others scholars have also focused on father-child relationships after divorce (e.g., Scott, Booth, King and Johnson 2007). A stepfather can develop a deep emotional connection with his stepchild even when the biological father is actively involved in the child's life. Moreover, for the benefit of the child, "some stepfathers are willing and able to develop civil, productive, and sometimes friendly relationships with the biological father" (Marsiglio and Hinojosa 2007:858).

Amato and Cheadle (2005) propose the intergenerational transmission of divorce. That is, that a divorce of their grandparents, through the parents, negatively affects the grandchildren's well being, by means of their parents, and thus increases their risk of divorce. However, the effect of divorce on boys can be mediated through their father (whether biological or step). Boys who feel close to their father felt less likely to divorce in the future (Risch, Jodl and Eccles 2004).

In November of 2004, *The Journal of Marriage and the Family* devoted a special issue to the topic of marriage and its future. Scholars note that the state of marriage has changed and that cohabitation and same-sex marriages have become viable options (Walker 2004). Marriage, although 'deinstitutionalized', remains important on a symbolic level; it is a meaningful system (Cherlin 2004; Gillis 2004). Unlike Western Europe the debate in the United States is value-laden. In European countries, the policies and political discussions have less to do with "what is best, cohabitation or marriage?", and are "more about issues concerning how best to support families, particularly in their endeavors to raise children, regardless of the marital status of their parents" (Kiernan 2004:980). Adams (2004) notes that marriage is an individual choice and given the high rate of remarriage, marriage is not rejected as an institution. He briefly discusses commuter marriages as "efforts to keep marriage alive, while not letting it stand in the way of individual goals" (p.1082).

Contemporary society is stressful for any type of family. In many instances, both parents have to work in order to pay the bills. There is an increase in women's labor force participation and Americans are working longer hours (Polatnick 2000). Divorced and widowed families face a loss of income and possibly a push toward poverty. As a result their children's health, well being, and educational opportunities may become compromised. Remarried families have the gigantic task of blending their families in situations when there are time constraints. Fathers, stepfathers, mothers and stepmothers need to have time to spend with their children instead of being pushed into a pressure cooker of balancing work and (step) family. Our society needs to be more geared toward the ideal context in which to raise children. The government should facilitate family arrangements that are beneficial for families and adopt policies that could alleviate the burden currently placed on all types of families by, for example, generously subsidizing parental leave and after school child care, and by making healthcare benefits for part-time workers mandatory. Further, I propose that the government expands the Family and Medical Leave Act in order to provide for families who are going through a divorce, and to provide for families who are newly formed blended families by giving precious time off to those families who clearly need these extra days.

Brotherson and Duncan (2004) suggest government intervention in terms of "...marriage promotion policies that set up strategies to counsel and educate both unmarried and married couples about the factors leading to more successful marriage and the benefits of marriage for couples and their children" (p. 466). My problem with their approach lies in the emphasis on marriage and the marital bond. In my perception, the focus of policies should be on couples with children (regardless of marital status) and I advocate government subsidized workshops, subsidized counseling and education (thereby making it financially feasible to attend) aimed at everyone who is part of a blended family. Strengthening family ties on an intergenerational level ((step)parent-adult child) and intra-generational level (adult siblings) should be the focus of government programs, not only for the well-being of those families, but also in light of the fact that the 'Baby Boomer' generation (those born between 1946 and 1964) is on the brink of retirement. Eventually, in the (near) future, this generation may require coordinated (family) care.

Given the fact that the blended family is projected to become the dominant family form by the year 2010 (Berger 1998), given the importance of family and family member's assistance, and given shortcomings in current scholarly research, I suggest that future research pertaining to this type of family will address feminist critiques (as outlined in chapter four) and incorporate qualitative research methods, preferably aimed at all individuals in blended sibling groups. Specifically, future research might prove fruitful in investigating the association between marital status and contact with siblings. I also encourage future research to determine if the effects of a larger group of full siblings are as substantial and persistent. Further studies may thus provide a more accurate kaleidoscope view of the current and future American family landscape.

REFERENCES

Adams, Bert N. 2004. "Families and Family Study in International Perspective." *Journal of Marriage and the Family* 66:1076-1088.

Adams, J. Stacy. 1965. "Inequity in Social Exchange." in *Advances in Experimental Social Psychology*, vol.2, edited by L. Berkowitz. New York: Academic Press.

Ahrons, Constance. 2004. *We're Still Family: What Grown Children Have to Say about Their Parents' Divorce*. New York: HarperCollins.

Allen, Katherine R. 2000. "A Conscious and Inclusive Family Studies." *Journal of Marriage and the Family* 62:4-15.

Amato, Paul R. and Jacob Cheadle. 2005. "The Long Reach of Divorce: Divorce and Child Well-Being across Three Generations." *Journal of Marriage and the Family* 67:191-206.

Amato, Paul R. and Frieda Fowler. 2002. "Parenting Practices, Child Adjustment, and Family Diversity." *Journal of Marriage and the Family* 64:703-716.

Amato, Paul R. and Denise Previti. 2003. "People's Reasons for Divorcing: Gender, Social Class, the Life Course, and Adjustment." *Journal of Family Issues* 24:602-626.

Anderson, Edward R. 1999. "Sibling, Half Sibling and Stepsibling Relationships in Remarried Families." *Monographs of the Society for Research in Child Development* 64:101-126.

Applewhite, Ashton. 1997. *Cutting Loose: Why Women Who End Their Marriages Do So Well*. New York: Harper Collins.

Baer, Judith. 2002. "Is Family Cohesion a Risk or Protective Factor During Adolescent Development?" *Journal of Marriage and the Family* 64:668-675.

Bahr, Kathleen Slaugh and Nancy Rollins Ahlander. 1996. "Morality, Feminism and Family Work: A Reply to Sanchez's Commentary." *Journal of Marriage and the Family* 58:520-526.

Ball, Derek and Peter Kivisto. 2006. "Couples Facing Divorce." Pp.145-161 in *Couples, Kids, and Family Life*, edited by Jaber F. Gubrium and James A. Holstein. New York; Oxford: Oxford University Press.

Baumrind, Diana. 1966. "Effects of Authoritative Parental Control on Child Behavior." *Child Development* 37:887-907.

-----. 1967. "Childcare Practices Anteceding Three Patterns of Preschool Behavior." *Genetic Psychology Monographs* 75:43-88.

Baxter, Leslie A., Dawn O. Braithwaite, Leah Bryant, and Amy Wagner. 2004. "Stepchildren's Perceptions of the Contradictions in Communication with Stepparents." *Journal of Social and Personal Relationships* 21:447-467.

Baydar, Nazli, April Greek, and Jeanne Brooks-Gunn. 1997. "A Longitudinal Study of the Effects of the Birth of a Sibling during the First 6 Years of Life." *Journal of Marriage and the Family* 59:939-956.

Baydar, Nazli, Patricia Hyle, and Jeanne Brooks-Gunn. 1997. "A Longitudinal Study of the Effects of the Birth of a Sibling during Preschool and Early Grade School Years." *Journal of Marriage and the Family* 59:957-965.

Beauvoir, Simone de. [1949] 1999. "Women as Other." Pp. 337-339 in *Social Theory: The Multicultural and Classic Readings*, edited by Charles Lemert. Boulder, CO: Westview Press.

Bedford, Victoria Hilkevitch. 1998. "Sibling Relationship Troubles and Well-Being in Middle and Old Age." *Family Relations* 47:369-376.

Bengtson, Vern L. and R.E.L. Roberts. 1991. "Intergenerational Solidarity in Aging Families: An Example of Formal Theory Construction." *Journal of Marriage and the Family* 53:856-870.

Bengtson, Vern, Roseann Giarrusso, J. Beth Mabry, and Merrill Silverstein. 2002. "Solidarity, Conflict and Ambivalence: Complementary or Competing Perspectives on Intergenerational Relationships." *Journal of Marriage and the Family* 64:568-576.

Berger, Roni. 1998. *Stepfamilies: a Multi-dimensional Perspective*. New York: Haworth Press.

Berscheid, Ellen. 1995. "Help Wanted: A Grand Theorist of Interpersonal Relationships, Sociologist or Anthropologist Preferred." *Journal of Social and Personal Relationships* 12:529-533.

Blau, Peter M. 1964. *Exchange and Power in Social Life*. New York: Wiley.

------. 1997. "On Limitations of Rational Choice Theory for Sociology." *American Sociologist* 28:16-22.

Blumstein, Philip and Peter Kollock. 1988. "Personal Relationships." *Annual Review of Sociology* 14:467-490.

Bohannan, Paul and Rosemary Erickson. 1978. "Stepping In." *Psychology Today* 11: 53, 54 and 59.

Booth, Alan and Paul R. Amato. 1994. "Parental Marital Quality, Parental Divorce, and Relations with Parents." *Journal of Marriage and the Family* 56:21-34.

Borrine, M. Lisa, Paul J. Handal, Nancy Y. Brown, and H. Russell Searight. 1991. "Family Conflict and Adolescent Adjustment in Intact, Divorced, and Blended Families." Journal of Family Psychology 59:753-755.

Boteach, Shmuley. 2008. *The Broken American Male: And How To Fix Him*. New York: St. Martin's Press.

Brody, Gene H., Zolinda Stoneman, and J. Kelly McCoy. 1994. "Contributions of Family Relationships and Child Temperaments to Longitudinal Variations in Sibling Relationship Quality and Sibling Relationship Styles." *Journal of Family Psychology* 8:274-286.

Brody, Gene H., Zolinda Stoneman, Trellis Smith, and Nicole Morgan Gibson. 1999. "Sibling Relationships in Rural African American Families." *Journal of Marriage and the Family* 61:1046-1057.

Brotherson, Sean E. and William C. Duncan. 2004. "Rebinding the Ties That Bind: Government Efforts to Preserve and Promote Marriage." *Family Relations* 53: 459-468.

Brown, Kathleen A. 1999. "The Savagely Fathered and Un-mothered World of the Communist Party, U.S.A.: Feminism, Maternalism, and "Mother Bloor"." *Feminist Studies* 25:537-570.

Buckle, Leslie, Gordon G. Gallup Jr., and Zachary A. Rodd. 1996. "Marriage as a Reproductive Contract: Patterns of Marriage, Divorce, and Remarriage." *Ethology and Sociobiology* 17:363-377.

Buss, David M. 1999. *Evolutionary Psychology: The New Science of the Mind*. Boston: Allyn and Bacon.

Buunk, Bram P., Alois Angleitner, Viktor Oubaid, and David M. Buss. 1996. "Sex Differences in Jealousy in Evolutionary and Cultural Perspective: Tests from the Netherlands, Germany, and the United States." *Psychological Science* 7:359-363.

Byfield, Link. 1999. "Even More Terrifying Than State-sponsored Feminism is State-sponsored Masculinity." *Report/ Newsmagazine* (Alberta edition) 26, November 22:4.

Carnoy, Martin. 1999. "The Family, Flexible Work and Social Cohesion at Risk." *International Labour Review* 138:411-428.

Chagnon, Napoleon A. [1977] 1983. *Yanomamo: The Fierce People*. New York: Holt, Rinehart and Winston.

Charmaz, Kathy. 2000. "Grounded Theory: Objectivist and Constructivist Methods." Pp. 509-535 in *Handbook of Qualitative Research*, edited by Norman K. Denzin and Yvonna S. Lincoln. Thousand Oaks, CA: Sage.

Cherlin, Andrew. 1978. "Remarriage as an Incomplete Institution." *The American Journal of Sociology* 84:634-650.

------. 1983. "Changing Family and Household: Contemporary Lessons from Historical Research." *Annual Review of Sociology* 9:51-66.

------. 2004. "The Deinstitutionalization of American Marriage." *Journal of Marriage and the Family* 66:848-861.

Chodorow, Nancy. [1978] 1999. "Gender Personality and the Reproduction of Mothering." Pp. 406-409 in *Social Theory: The Multicultural and Classic Readings*, edited by Charles Lemert. Boulder, CO: Westview Press.

Cicirelli, Victor G. 1994. "Sibling Relationships in Cross-cultural Perspective." *Journal of Marriage and the Family* 56: 7-20.

------. 1995. *Sibling Relationships across the Life Span*. New York: Plenum Press.

Clarke, Sally C. 1995. "Advance Report of Final Divorce Statistics, 1989 and 1990." *Monthly Vital Statistics Report* 43 (9 – supplement).

Coleman, Marilyn, Lawrence Ganong, and Susan M. Cable. 1997. "Beliefs about Women's Intergenerational Family Obligations to Provide Support Before and After Divorce and Remarriage." *Journal of Marriage and the Family* 9:165-176.

Coleman, Marilyn and Lawrence H. Ganong. 2000. "Changing Families, Changing Responsibilities?" *National Forum: The Phi Kappa Phi Journal* 80:34-37.

Comte, Auguste. 1975. *Selections: Auguste Comte and Positivism*, edited by G. Lenzer. New York: Harper & Row.

Connides, Ingrid Arnet and Lori D. Campbell. 1995. "Closeness, Confiding, and Contact Among Siblings in Middle and Late Adulthood." *Journal of Family Issues* 16:722-745.

Cooley, Charles Horton (1961). "The Social Self." Pp. 822-828 in *Theories of Society: Foundations of Modern Sociological Theory*, edited by T. Parsons, E. Shils, K.D. Naegele and J.R. Pitts. New York: Free Press.

Coontz, Stephanie. 1992. *The Way We Never Were: American Families and the Nostalgia Trap*. New York: Basic Books.

------. 1997. *The Way We Really Are: Coming to Terms with America's Changing Families*. New York: Basic Books.

------. 2000. "Marriage: Then and Now." *National Forum: The Phi Kappa Phi Journal* 80:10-15.

------. 2005. *Marriage, A History: How Love Conquered Marriage*. New York: Penguin Books.

Coser, Rose Laub. 2004. "The Family: Its Structure and Functions." Pp. 13-21 in *Families and Society: Classic and Contemporary Readings,* edited by Scott Coltrane. Belmont, CA: Wadsworth.

Cumming, Edward and D.M. Schneider. 1961. "Sibling Solidarity: A Property of American Kinship." *American Anthropologist* 63:498-507.

Cutrona, Carolyn E. 2004. "A Psychological Perspective: Marriage and the Social Provisions of Relationships. *Journal of Marriage and the Family* 66:992-999.

Daly, Martin, Margo Wilson, and Suzanne J. Weghorst. 1982. "Male Sexual Jealousy." *Ethology and Sociobiology* 3:11-27.

Daly, Martin and Margo I. Wilson. 1982. "Whom Are Newborn Babies Said to Resemble?" *Ethology and Sociobiology* 3:69-78.

Daly, Martin and Margo Wilson.1998. *The Truth about Cinderella: a Darwinian View of Parental Love*. New Haven, CT: Yale University Press.

Daniels, Denise.1986. "Differential Experiences of Siblings in the Same Family as Predictors of Adolescent Sibling Personality Differences." *Journal of Personality and Social Psychology* 51:339-346.

Davis, Jennifer Nerissa. 1997. "Birth Order, Sibship Size, and Status in Modern Canada." *Human Nature* 8:205-230.

Davis, Jennifer Nerissa and Martin Daly. 1997. "Evolutionary Theory and the Human Family." *The Quarterly Review of Biology* 72:407-435.

Deal, James E., Charles F. Halverson, and Karen S. Wampler. 1994. "Sibling Similarity as an Individual Differences Variable: Within-Family Measures of Shared Environment." Pp. 205-218 in *Separate Social Worlds of Siblings: The Impact of Nonshared Environment on Development*, edited by E.M. Hetherington, D. Reiss, and R. Plomin. Hillsdale (etc.): Erlbaum.

Dey, Ian. 1999. *Grounding Grounded Theory: Guidelines for Qualitative Inquiry.* San Diego, CA: Academic Press.

Dillman, D.A. 1978. *Mail and Telephone Surveys: The Total Design Method.* New York: Wiley.

Donovan, Josephine. 1988. *Feminist Theory: The Intellectual Traditions of American Feminism.* New York: Ungar.

Dorfman, Lorraine T. and Carol E. Mertens. 1990. "Kinship Relations in Retired Rural Men and Women." *Family Relations* 39:166-173.

Duberman, Lucile. 1973. "Step-Kin Relationships." *Journal of Marriage and the Family* 35:283-292.

Dunn, Judy. 1988. "Annotation: Sibling Influences on Childhood Development." *Journal of Child Psychology and Psychiatry* 29:119-127.

Dunn, Judy and Carol Kendrick. 1982. *Siblings: Love, Envy and Understanding.* Cambridge, MA: Harvard University Press.

Dunn, Judy and Robert Plomin. 1990. *Separate Lives: Why Siblings Are So Different.* New York: Basic Books.

Dunn, Judy and Robert Plomin. 1991. "Why Are Siblings So Different? The Significance of Differences in Sibling Experiences within the Family." *Family Process* 30:271-283.

Dunn, Judy and Shirley McGuire. 1994. "Young Children's Nonshared Experiences: A Summary of Studies in Cambridge and Colorado." Pp. 111-128 in *Separate Social Worlds of Siblings: The Impact of Nonshared Environment on Development*, edited by E. Mavis Hetherington, D. Reiss, and R. Plomin. Hillsdale (etc.): Erlbaum.

Durkheim, Emile. 1972. *Emile Durkheim: Selected Writings.* Translated by Anthony Giddens. Edited and with an introduction by Anthony Gidddens. Cambridge; New York: Cambridge University Press.

------. [1897,1951] 1963. *Suicide: A Study in Sociology.* Translated by John Spaulding and George Simpson. Edited and with an introduction by George Simpson. Glencoe: The Free Press.

Dworkin, Andrea. [1981] 1992. "Pornography: Men Possessing Women." Pp. 83-86 in *Modern Feminisms: Political, Literary, Cultural*, edited by Maggie Humm. New York: Colombia University Press.

Elman, Cheryl and Andrew S. London. 2001. "Sociohistorical and Demographic Perspectives on U.S. Remarriage in 1910." *Social Science History* 25:407-447.

Emery, Robert E. 1988. *Marriage, Divorce, and Children's Adjustment.* Newbury Park, CA: Sage.

Engels, Friedrich. [1884, 1892]1942. *The Origin of the Family, Private Property and the State: in the Light of the Researches of Lewis H. Morgan.* New York: International Publishers.

Eriksen, Shelley and Naomi Gerstel. 2002. "A Labor of Love or Labor Itself: Care Work among Adult Brothers and Sisters." *Journal of Family Issues* 23:836-856.

ERS Staff Report.1995. "Family Structures of Children in the United States." *ERS Spectrum* 13:39-45.

Euler, Harald A. and Barbara Weitzel. 1996. "Discriminative Grandparental Solicitude as Reproductive Strategy." *Human Nature* 7:39-59.

Euler, Harald A., Sabrine Hoier, and Percy A. Rohde. 2001. "Relationship-Specific Closeness of Intergenerational Family Ties: Findings from Evolutionary Psychology and Implications for Models of Cultural Transmission." *Journal of Cross-Cultural Psychology* 32:147-158.

Fagan, Jay and Marina Barnett. 2003. "The Relationship Between Maternal Gatekeeping, Paternal Competence, Mothers' Attitudes About the Father Role, and Father Involvement." *Journal of Family Issues* 24:1020-1043.

Fan, C. Simon and Hon-Kwong Lui. 2004. "Extramarital Affairs, Marital Satisfaction and Divorce: Evidence From Hong Kong." *Contemporary Economic Policy* 22:442-452.

Farber, Bernard. 1973. "Comments on Rosenberg and Anspach, Sibling Solidarity in the Working Class." *Journal of Marriage and the Family* 35: 177.

Federal Interagency Forum on Child and Family Statistics. 2007. *America's Children: Key National Indicators of Well-Being.* Washington, DC: United States Government Printing Office. Retrieved June 15, 2008 (http://www.childstats.gov/americaschildren/famsoc1.asp).

Feinberg, Mark and E. Mavis Hetherington. 2001. "Differential Parenting as a Within-Family Variable." *Journal of Family Psychology* 15:22-37.

Festinger, Leon. 1954. "A Theory of Social Comparison Processes." *Human Relations* 7:117-140.

Filinson, Rachel. 1986. "Relationships in Stepfamilies: An Examination of Alliances." *Journal of Comparative Family Studies* 17:43-61.

Fox, Greer L. and Velma McBride Murray. 2000. "Gender and Families: Feminist Perspectives and Family Research." *Journal of Marriage and the Family* 62:1160-1172.

Foucault, Michel. 1978. *The History of Sexuality; volume 1: An Introduction.* Translated from the French by Robert Hurley. New York: Pantheon Books.

Freud, Sigmund. [1930] 1961. *Civilization and its Discontents.* Translated and edited by James Strachey. New York: Norton.

------. [1933] 1965. *New Introductory Lectures on Psychoanalysis.* Translated and edited by James Strachey. New York: Norton.

Frey, James H. 1989. *Survey Research by Telephone*. Newbury Park, CA: Sage.
Friedan, Betty. [1963] 1999. "The Problem That Has No Name." Pp. 356-359 in *Social Theory: The Multicultural and Classic Readings*, edited by Charles Lemert. Boulder, CO: Westview Press.
Friedman, Debra and Michael Hechter. 1990. "The Comparative Advantages of Rational Choice Theory." Pp. 214-229 in *Frontiers of Social Theory: The New Synthesis*, edited by George Ritzer. New York: Colombia University Press.
Furman, Wyndol and Duane Buhrmester. 1985. "Children's Perceptions of the Qualities of Sibling Relationships." *Child Development* 56:448-461.
Furstenberg, Frank F. and Julien O. Teitler. 1994. "Reconsidering the Effects of Marital Disruption: What Happens to Children of Divorce in Early Adulthood?" *Journal of Family Issues* 15:173-190.
Gaalen, Ruben I. Van and Pearl A. Dykstra. 2006. "Solidarity and Conflict between Adult Children and Parents: A Latent Class Analysis." *Journal of Marriage and Family* 68: 947-960.
Gallagher, Maggie 1997. "New Emphasis on Family is Replacing Feminism." *Human Events* 53:13.
Galvin, Kathleen M., Carma L. Bylund, and Bernard J. Brommel. 2004. *Family, Communication : Cohesion and Change*. 6th ed. Boston: Pearson.
Ganong, Lawerence H. and Marilyn Coleman. 1988. "Do Mutual Children Cement Bonds in Stepfamilies?" *Journal of Marriage and the Family* 50: 687-698.
Ganong, Lawrence H. and Marilyn Coleman. 1994. *Remarried Family Relationships*. Thousand Oaks, CA; London, England: Sage.
Gardels, Nathan. 1998. "The New Frontier of Feminism: Busting the Masculine Mystique." *NPQ: New Perspective Quarterly* 15:57-60.
Gaulin, Steven J.C., Donald H. McBurney and Stephanie L. Brakeman-Wartell. 1997. "Matrilateral Biases in the Investment of Aunts and Uncles: A Consequence and Measure of Paternity Uncertainty." *Human Nature* 8:139-151.
Gay, Peter. 1988. *Freud: A Life for Our Time*. New York; London: Norton.
Geary, David C. 2000. "Evolution and Proximate Expression of Human Paternal Investment." *Psychological Bulletin* 126:55-77.
Georgas, James, Sophia Christakopoulou, Ybe H. Poortinga, Alois Angleitner, Robin Goodwin, and Neophytos Charalambous. 1997. "The Relationship of Family Bonds to Family Structure and Function across Cultures." *Journal of Cross-Cultural Psychology* 28:303-320.
Gerth, Hans H. and C. Wright Mills, eds. 1958. *From Max Weber: Essays in Sociology*. New York: Oxford University Press.
Giddens, Anthony, ed. 1972. *Emile Durkheim: Selected Writings*. Cambridge; New York: Cambridge University Press.

Gillis, John R. 2004. "Marriages of the Mind." *Journal of Marriage and the Family* 66:988-991.

Gilmore, David D. 1982. "Anthropology of the Mediterranean Area." *Annual Review of Anthropology* 11:175-205.

Glenn, Norval. 1997. *Closed Hearts, Closed Minds: The Textbook Story of Marriage.* New York: Institute for American Values

Gottman, John M., James Coan, Sybil Carrere, and Catherine Swanson. 1998. "Predicting Marital Happiness and Stability from Newlywed Interactions." *Journal of Marriage and the Family* 60:5-22.

Greer, Jane and Edward Myers. 1992. *Adult Sibling Rivalry: Understanding the Legacy of Childhood.* New York: Crown Publishers.

Hackstaff, Karla B. 1999. *Marriage in a Culture of Divorce.* Philadelphia, PA: Temple University Press.

Hamilton, W. 1964. "The Genetic Evolution of Social Behavior I and II." *Journal of Theoretical Biology* 7:1-52.

Hammersley, Martyn. 1989. *The Dilemma of Qualitative Method: Herbert Blumer and the Chicago Tradition.* London, England: Routledge.

Handel, Gerald 1986. "Beyond Sibling Rivalry: An Empirically Grounded Theory of Sibling Relationships." Pp. 105-122 in *Sociological Studies of Child Development: A Research Annual,* edited by Patricia. A. Adler, Peter Adler and Nancy Mandell. Greenwich, CT; London, England: JAI Press.

Harris, Elise. 2000. "Can Marriage Be Saved?: An Unsentimental Case For Matrimony." *Lingua Franca: The Review of Academic Life* 10 (8):26-33.

Hartmann, Heidi. [1976] 1992. "Capitalism, Patriarchy, and Job Segregation by Sex." Pp. 99-104 in *Modern Feminisms: Political, Literary, Cultural,* edited by Maggie Humm. New York: Colombia University Press.

Hetherington, E. Mavis. 1988. "Parents, Children, and Siblings: Six Years After Divorce." Pp. 311-331 in *Relationships within Families: Mutual Influences,* edited by Robert A. Hinde and Joan Stevenson-Hinde. Oxford: Clarendon Press.

------. 1994. "Siblings, Family Relationships, and Child Development: Introduction." *Journal of Family Psychology* 8:251-253.

------. 2003. "Social Support and the Adjustment of Children in Divorced and Remarried Families." *Childhood* 10:217-236.

Hetherington, E. Mavis and John Kelly. 2002. *For Better or For Worse: Divorce Reconsidered.* New York; London: Norton.

Hochschild, Arlie. 1997. *The Time Bind: When Work Becomes Home and Home Becomes Work.* New York: Metropolitan Books.

Hochschild, Arlie [1997] 1999. "Working Women in the Time Bind." Pp. 654-657 in *Social Theory: The Multicultural and Classic Readings,* edited by Charles Lemert. Boulder, CO: Westview Press.

Hofstede, Geert. 1991. *Cultures and Organizations: Software of the Mind.* London, England: McGraw-Hill.

Homans, George C. 1950. *The Human Group*. New York: Harcourt, Brace and World.

Homans, George C. [1961] 1974. *Social Behavior: Its Elementary Forms*. New York (etc.): Harcourt Brace Jovanovich.

------. 1969. "The Sociological Relevance of Behaviorism." Pp. 1-24 in *Behavioral Sociology: The Experimental Analysis of Social Process*, edited by R. L. Burgess and D. Bushell. New York: Colombia University Press.

House, James, Debra Umberson, and K.R. Landis. 1988. "Structures and Processes of Social Support." *Annual Review of Sociology* 14:293-318.

Hoyt, Danny R. and Nicholas Babchuck. 1983. "Adult Kinship Networks: The Selective Formation of Intimate ties with Kin." *Social Forces* 62:84-101.

Hrdy, Sara B. 1987. "Sex-Biased Parental Investment among Primates and Other Mammals: A Critical Evaluation of the Trivers-Willard Hypothesis." Pp. 97-147 in *Child Abuse and Neglect: Biosocial Dimensions*, edited by R.J. Gelles and J.B. Lancaster. New York: de Gruyter.

ICPSR. 2005. "GSS About: Introduction to the GSS." Ann Arbor, MI: ICPSR. Retrieved May 24, 2005 (http://webapp.icpsr.umich.edu/GSS/about/gss/about.htm).

Ihinger-Tallman, Marilyn. 1987a. "The American Family: A Poem". *Journal of Family Issues* 8:444-447.

------. 1987b. "Sibling and Stepsibling Bonding in Stepfamilies." Pp. 164-182 in *Remarriage and Stepparenting: Current Research and Theory*, edited by Kay Pasley and Marilyn Ihinger-Tallman. New York; London, England: Guilford Press.

------. 1988. "Research on Stepfamilies." *Annual Review of Sociology* 14:25-48.

Ihinger-Tallman, Marilyn and Kay Pasley.1997. "Stepfamilies in 1984 and Today – A Scholarly Perspective." *Marriage and Family Review* 26:19-40.

Iulina, N.S. and James P. Scanlan. 1996. "Women, the Family and Society: Discussions in the Feminist Thought of the United States." *Russian Social Science Review* 37:71- 94.

Jankowiak, William and Monique Diderich 2000. "Sibling Solidarity in a Polygamous Community in the USA: Unpacking Inclusive Fitness." *Evolution and Human Behavior* 21:125-139.

Jones, Ann C. 2003. "Reconstructing the Stepfamily: Old Myths, New Stories." *Social Work: Journal of the National Association of Social Workers* 48: 228-236.

Jorgensen, Danny L. 1989. *Participant Observation: A Methodology for Human Studies*. Newbury Park, CA: Sage.

Keller, Heidi. 2000. "Human Parent-Child Relationships from an Evolutionary Perspective." *American Behavioral Scientist* 43:957-969.

Kerig, Patricia K. 1995. "Triangles in the Family Circle: Effects of Family Structure on Marriage, Parenting, and Child Adjustment." *Journal of Family Psychology* 9:28-43.

Kiernan, Kathleen. 2004. "Redrawing the Boundaries of Marriage." *Journal of Marriage and the Family* 66:980-987.

King, Valerie. 2002. "Parental Divorce and Interpersonal Trust in Adult Offspring." *Journal of Marriage and the Family* 64:642-656.

Knight, George P. and Chia-Chen Chao. 1991. "Cooperative, Competitive, and Individualistic Social Values among 8- to 12-Year-Old Siblings, Friends, and Acquaintances." *Personality and Social Psychology Bulletin* 17:201-211.

Koch, Helen L. 1960. "The Relation of Certain Formal Attributes of Siblings to Attitudes Held Toward Each Other and Toward Their Parents." *Monographs of the Society for Research in Child Development* 25(4):3-124.

Kramer, Laurie and John M. Gottman. 1992. "Becoming a Sibling: With a Little Help from My Friends." *Developmental Psychology* 28:685-699.

Kreider, Rose M. and Jason M. Fields. 2001. "Number, Timing, and Duration of Marriages and Divorces: Fall 1996." *Current Population Reports*, P70-80. Washington DC: U.S. Census Bureau.

Kurdek, Lawrence A. and Mark Fine. 1995. "Mothers, Fathers, Stepfathers, and Siblings as Providers of Supervision, Acceptance, and Autonomy to Young Adolescents." *Journal of Family Psychology* 9:95-99.

Kurland, Jeffrey A. 1979. "Paternity, Mother's Brother and Human Sociality." Pp. 145-180 in *Evolutionary Biology and Human Social Behavior: An Anthropological Perspective*, edited by Napoleon A. Chagnon and William Irons. North Scituate, MA: Duxbury Press.

Kurz, Demie. 1995. *For Richer, For Poorer: Mothers Confront Divorce*. New York; London: Routledge.

Lalumière, Martin L., Vernon L. Quinsey, and Wendy M. Craig. 1996. "Why Children From the Same Family Are So Different From One Another: A Darwinian Note." *Human Nature* 7:281-290.

Lasch, Christopher. 1975. *Haven in a Heartless World: The Family Besieged*. New York: Basic Books.

------. [1977] 1999. "The Moynihan Report: Rethinking Family." Pp. 400 - 406 in *Social Theory: The Multicultural and Classic Readings*, edited by Charles Lemert. Boulder, CO: Westview Press.

Lawton, Leora, Merrill Silverstein, and Vern Bengtson. 1994. "Affection, Social Contact and Geographic Distance between Adult Children and Their Parents." *Journal of Marriage and the Family* 56:57-68.

Lee, Thomas R., Jay A. Mancini, and Joseph W. Maxwell. 1990. "Sibling Relations in Adulthood: Contact Patterns and Motivations." *Journal of Marriage and the Family* 52:431-440.

Leigh, Geoffrey K. 1982. "Kinship Interaction over the Family Life Span." *Journal of Marriage and the Family* 44:197-208.
Leon, Kim and Erin Angst. 2005. "Portrayals of Stepfamilies in Film: Using Media Images in Remarriage Education." *Family Relations* 54:3-23.
Littlefield, Christine H. and J. Philippe Rushton. 1986. "When a Child Dies: The Sociobiology of Bereavement." *Journal of Personality and Social Psychology* 51:707-802.
Lüscher, Kurt. 2002. "Intergenerational Ambivalence: Further Steps in Theory and Research." *Journal of Marriage and the Family* 64:585-593.
Mace, Ruth. 1996. "Biased Parental Investment and Reproductive Success in Gabbra Pastoralists." *Behavioral Ecology and Sociobiology* 38:75-81.
MacKinnon, Carol E. 1989. "An Observational Investigation of Sibling Interactions in Married and Divorced Families." *Developmental Psychology* 25:36-44.
McChesney, Kay Young and Vern L. Bengtson. 1988. "Solidarity, Integration, and Cohesion in Families: Concepts and Theories." Pp. 15-30 in *Measurement of Intergenerational Relations*, edited by David J. Mangen, Vern L. Bengtson, and Pierre H. Landry. Newbury Park, CA: Sage.
Marshall, Catherine and Gretchen B. Rossman. 1989. *Designing Qualitative Research*. Newbury Park, CA: Sage.
Marsiglio, William. 2004. "When Stepfathers Claim Stepchildren: A Conceptual Analysis." *Journal of Marriage and the Family* 66:22-39.
Marsiglio, William and Ramon Hinojosa. 2007. "Managing the Multifather Family: Stepfathers as Father Allies." *Journal of Marriage and Family* 69: 845-862.
Matthews, Sarah H. 2002. *Sisters and Brothers/Daughters and Sons: Meeting the Needs of Old Parents*. Bloomington, Indiana: Unlimited Publishing.
Meertens, R.W. and J. von Grumbkow, eds. 1988. *Social Psychology* (in Dutch). Groningen, The Netherlands: Wolters-Noordhoff.
Miller, Susan J., David J. Hickson, and David C. Wilson. 1996. "Decision-Making in Organizations." Pp. 293-312 in *Handbook of Organization Studies*, edited by Stewart R. Clegg, Cynthia Hardy, and Walter R. Nord. London, England: Sage.
Miner, Sonia and Peter Uhlenberg. 1997. "Intragenerational Proximity and the Social Role of Sibling Neighbors after Midlife." *Family Relations* 46:145-153.
Musun-Miller, Linda. 1993. "Sibling Status Effects: Parents' Perceptions of Their Own Children." *The Journal of Genetic Psychology* 154:189-198.
Neuman, W. Lawrence. 2000. *Social Research Methods: Qualitative and Quantitative Approaches*. Boston: Allyn and Bacon.
Neyer, Franz J. and Frieder R. Lang. 2003. "Blood is Thicker than Water: Kinship Orientation across Adulthood." *Journal of Personality and Social Psychology* 84:310-321.

Parkman, Allen M. 2004. "The Importance of Gifts in Marriage." *Economic Inquiry* 42:483-495.

Parsons, Talcott. 1943. "The Kinship System of the Contemporary United States." *American Anthropologist* 45:22-38.

Pasley, Kay and Marilyn Ihinger-Tallman. 1985. "Portraits of Stepfamily Life in Popular Literature: 1940-1980." *Family Relations* 34:527-534.

Pasley, B. Kay and Marilyn Ihinger Tallman. 1989. "Boundary Ambiguity in Remarriage: Does Ambiguity Differentiate Degree of Marital Adjustment and Integration?" *Family Relations* 38:46-52.

Peterson, Richard R. 1996. "A Re-evaluation of the Economic Consequences of Divorce." *American Sociological Review* 61:528-536.

Pfaller, Joan, Mark Kiselica, and Lawrence Gerstein. 1998. "Attachment Style and Family Dynamics in Young Adults." *Journal of Counseling Psychology* 45:353-357.

Piercy, Kathleen. 1998. "Theorizing About Family Caregiving: The Role of Responsibility." Journal of Marriage and the Family 60:109-118.

Polatnitck, M. Rivka. 2000. Working Parents. *National Forum: The Phi Kappa Phi Journal* 80:38-41.

Popenoe, David. 1996. *Life Without Father: Compelling New Evidence that Fatherhood and Marriage Are Indispensable for the Good of Children and Society.* New York: Martin Kessler Books.

Pulakos, Joan. 1990. "Correlations between Family Environment and Relationships of Young Adult Siblings." *Psychological Reports* 67:1283-1286.

Reiss, David, Robert Plomin, E. Mavis Hetherington, G.W. Howe, Michael J. Rovine, A. Tyron, and M.S. Hagan. 1994. "The Separate Worlds of Teenage Siblings: An Introduction to the Study of the Nonshared Environment and Adolescent Development." Pp. 63-109 in *Separate Social Worlds of Siblings: The Impact of Nonshared Environment on Development*, edited by E.M. Hetherington, D. Reiss, and R. Plomin. Hillsdale, NJ: Erlbaum.

Reynolds, H.T. 1977. *Analysis of Nominal Data*. London, England: Sage Publications.

Riley, Pamela J. and Gary Kiger. 1999. "Moral Discourse on Domestic Labor: Gender, Power, and Identity in Families." *Social Science Journal* 36:541-548.

Risch, Sharon C., Kathleen M. Jodl, and Jacquelynne S. Eccles. 2004. "Role of Father-Adolescent Relationship in Shaping Adolescents' Attitudes toward Divorce." *Journal of Marriage and the Family* 66:46-58.

Rogers, Stacy J. 2004. "Dollars, Dependency, and Divorce: Four Perspectives on the Role of Wives' Income." *Journal of Marriage and the Family* 66:59-74.

Rosenberg, George S. and Donald F. Anspach. 1973. "Sibling Solidarity in the Working Class." *Journal of Marriage and the Family* 35:108-113.

Rosenthal, Carolyn J. 1985. "Kinkeeping in the Familial Division of Labor." *Journal of Marriage and the Family* 47:965-974.

Rubin, Beth. A. 1996. *Shifts in the Social Contract: Understanding Change in American Society*. Thousand Oaks, CA: Pine Forge Press.

Salmon, Catherine A. and Martin Daly. 1996. "On the Importance of Kin Relations to Canadian Women and Men." *Ethology and Sociobiology* 17: 289-297.

Salmon, Catherine A. and Martin Daly.1998. "Birth Order and Familial Sentiment: Middleborns Are Different." *Evolution and Human Behavior* 19:299-312.

Sanchez, Laura. 1996. "Feminism, Family Work, and Moral Discourse: A Comment on Ahlander and Bahr's "Beyond Drudgery, Power and Equity." *Journal of Marriage and the Family* 58:514-520.

Sarkisian, Natalia and Naomi Gerstel. 2008. "Till Marriage Do Us Part: Adult Children's Relationships with Their Parents." *Journal of Marriage and Family* 70: 360-376.

Schlegel, Alice and Herbert Barry. 1991. *Adolescence: An Anthropological Inquiry*. New York: Free Press.

Schmeekckle, Maria. 2007. "Gender Dynamics in Stepfamilies: Adult Stepchildren's Views." *Journal of Marriage and Family* 69: 174-189.

Schor, Juliet B. 1991. *The Overworked American: The Unexpected Decline of Leisure*. New York: Basic Books.

Scott, Mindy, Alan Booth, Valerie King, and David R. Johnson. 2007. "Postdivorce Father-Adolescent Closeness. *Journal of Marriage and Family* 69: 1194-1209.

Shanahan, Lilly, Susan M. McHale, Ann C. Crouter, and D. Wayne Osgood. 2008 "Linkages between Parents' Differential Treatment, Youth Depressive Symptoms, and Sibling Relationships." *Journal of Marriage and Family* 70: 480-494.

Shavitt, Yossi and Jennifer L. Pierce. 1991. "Sibship Size and Educational Attainment in Nuclear and Extended Families: Arabs and Jews in Israel." *American Sociological Review* 56:321-330.

Silverstein, Merrill and Vern L. Bengtson. 1997. "Intergenerational Solidarity and the Structure of Adult Child-Parent Relationships in American Families." *American Journal of Sociology* 103:429-460.

Simmel, George. 1984. *George Simmel: On Women, Sexuality and Love*. New Haven: Yale University Press.

Simpson, Bob. 1998. *Changing Families: An Ethnographic Approach to Divorce and Separation*. Oxford; New York: Berg

Skeen, Patsy, Bryan E. Robinson, and Carol Flake-Hobson. 1984. "Blended Families: Overcoming the Cinderella Myth." *Young Children* 39:64-74.

Smith, Dorothy. [1974] 1999. "Knowing a Society from within: A Woman's Standpoint." Pp. 388-390 in *Social Theory: The Multicultural and Classic Readings*, edited by Charles Lemert. Boulder, CO: Westview Press.

South, Scott J., Kyle D. Crowder, and Katherine Trent. 1998. "Children's Residential Mobility and Neighborhood Environment Following Parental Divorce and Remarriage. " *Social Forces* 77:667-693.

Spanier, Graham B. and Frank F. Furstenberg. 1987. "Remarriage and Reconstituted Families." Pp. 419-434 in *Handbook of Marriage and the Family*, edited by Marvin B. Sussman and Suzanne K. Steinmetz. New York; London: Plenum Press.

Spigelman, Gabriella, Ami Spigelman, and Irmelin L. Englesson. 1992. "Analysis of Family Drawings: A Comparison between Children from Divorce and Non-Divorce Families." *Journal of Divorce and Remarriage* 18:31-54.

Spitze, Glenda and John R. Logan. 1991. "Sibling Structure and Intergenerational Relations." *Journal of Marriage and the Family* 53:871-884.

SPSS Inc. 1997. *SPSS Base 10.0 Applications Guide*. Chicago: SPSS Inc.

Stacey, Judith [1996] 1999. "The Post-Modern Family." Pp. 647-653 in *Social Theory: The Multicultural and Classic Readings*, edited by Charles Lemert. Boulder, CO: Westview Press.

Stocker, Clare M. and Susan M. McHale. 1992. "The Nature and Family Correlates of Preadolescents' Perceptions of Their Sibling Relationship." *Journal of Social and Personal Relationships* 9:179-195.

Stocker, Clare M., Richard P. Lanthier, and Wyndol Furman. 1997. "Sibling Relationships in Early Adulthood." *Journal of Family Psychology* 11:210-221.

Sulloway, Frank J. 1996. *Born to Rebel*. NewYork: Pantheon Books.

------.1998. "Darwinian Virtues." *The New York Review of Books* 45:34, 36-40.

Sweeney, Megan M. 1997. "Remarriage of Women and Men after Divorce: The Role of Socioeconomic Prospects." *Journal of Family Issues* 18:479-502.

Teachman, Jay. 2008. "Complex Life Course Patterns and the Risk of Divorce in Second Marriages." Journal of Marriage and Family 70: 294-305.

U.S. Bureau of the Census 1997. *Statistical Abstract of the United States: 1997* (117th edition). Washington, DC (pp -----------------).

United States Department of Labor, Bureau of Labor Statistics. 2005. "News". Retrieved June 16, 2005 (http://www.bls.gov/news.release/pdf/famee.pdf).

Voorpostel, Marieke and Tanja Van Der Lippe. 2007. "Support between Siblings and between Friends: Two Worlds Apart?" *Journal of Marriage and Family* 69: 1271-1282.

Voorpostel, Marieke and Rosemary Blieszner. 2008. "Intergenerational Solidarity and Support between Adult Siblings." *Journal of Marriage and Family* 70: 157-167.

Waite, Linda J., Don Browning, William J. Doherty, Maggie Gallagher, Ye Luo, and Scott M. Stanley. 2002. *Does Divorce Make People Happy? Findings from a Study of Unhappy Marriages*. New York: Institute for American Values.

Walker, Alexis. 2004. "A Symposium on Marriage and its Future. *Journal of Marriage and the Family* 66:843-847.

Wallerstein, Judith S. and Sandra Blakeslee. [1989] 1990. *Second Chances: Men, Women, and Children a Decade after Divorce*. New York: Ticknor and Fields.

Weaver, Shannon E., Marilyn Coleman, and Lawrence Ganong. 2003. "The Sibling Relationship in Young Adulthood: Sibling Functions and Relationship Perceptions as Influenced by Sibling Pair Composition." *Journal of Family Issues* 24:245-263.

Weber, Marianne. [1912] 2003. "Authority and Autonomy in Marriage", Translation with Introduction and Commentary by Craig R. Bermingham. *Sociological Theory* 21:85-102.

White, Lynn. 1994. "Growing Up With Single Parents and Stepparents: Long-Term Effects on Family Solidarity." *Journal of Marriage and the Family* 56: 935-948.

------. 1998. "Who's Counting? Quasi-Facts and Stepfamilies in Reports of Number of Siblings." *Journal of Marriage and the Family* 60:725-733.

------. 2001. "Sibling Relationships over the Life Course: A Panel Analysis." *Journal of Marriage and the Family* 63:555-568.

White, Lynn K. and Agnes Riedmann. 1992a. "Ties among Adult Siblings." *Social Forces* 71:85-102.

White, Lynn K. and Agnes Riedmann. 1992b. "When the Brady Bunch Grows up: Step/ Half- and Full Sibling Relationships in Adulthood." *Journal of Marriage and the Family* 54:197-208.

White, Lynn K. and Stacy J. Rogers. 1997. "Strong Support but Uneasy Relationships: Coresidence and Adult Children's Relationships with their Parents." *Journal of Marriage and the Family* 59:62-76.

White, Lynn and Joan G. Gilbreth. 2001. "When Children Have Two Fathers: Effects of Relationships with Stepfathers and Noncustodial Fathers on Adolescent Outcomes." *Journal of Marriage and the Family* 63:155-167.

Whiteside, Mary F. 1989. "Family Rituals as a Key to Kinship Connections in Remarried Families." *Family Relations* 38:34-39.

Wilson, Edward Osborne. 1975. *Sociobiology: the New Synthesis*. Cambridge: Harvard University Press.

Wolff, Kurt H., ed. 1950. *The Sociology of Georg Simmel*. New York: The Free Press.

INDEX

Adams, Bert N., 136
Adams, J. Stacy, 23, 51-52
Affectual solidarity, 11-12, 65,76, 102-103, 114-117, 130-132
Ahlander, Nancy Rollins, 35
Ahrons, Constance, 7
Allen, Katherine R., 11, 34, 66-67
Allies, 28, 60-61
Altruism, 28, 47, 57, 87
   Kin, 57, 87
   Reciprocal, 28, 47, 57, 87
Amato, Paul R., 59, 80, 135
Ambiguity, 83, 86-87, 91
Ambivalence, 10, 83, 85-87, 134
Anderson, Edward R., 124, 127
Angleitner, Alois, 45, 55
Angst, Erin, 40
Anspach, Donald F., 10, 58, 112
Applewhite, Ashton, 7
Associational solidarity, 11, 12, 65, 76, 102-104, 114, 117-119, 125, 130, 131, 133
Attachment theory, 41-42
Babchuck, Nicholas, 22, 130
Baer, Judith, 100
Bahr, Kathleen Slaugh, 35
Ball, Derek, 8
Barnett, Marina, 135
Barry, Herbert, 61
Baxter, Leslie A., 6, 86
Baumrind, Diana, 73
Baydar, Nazli, 47-48
Beauvoir, Simone De, 32-33
Bedford, Victoria Hilkevitch, 120
Bengtson, Vern L., 10, 11, 56, 57, 76, 85
Berger, Roni, 5, 6, 137

Berscheid, Ellen, 62
Birth order, 42, 43, 47, 51, 97, 124
Blakeslee, Sandra, 7, 135
Blau, Peter M., 24-25, 27, 51, 52
Bleuler, Eugen, 86
Blieszner, Rosemary, 125
Bloor, Ella, 29-31, 33
Blumer, Herbert, 69
Blumstein, Philip, 22
Bohannan, Paul, 4, 6, 60
Booth, Alan, 59, 135
Borrine, M. Lisa, 91
Boteach, Shmuley, 8
Boundary ambiguity, 86-87, 91
Brady Bunch, 5, 6
Braithwaite, Dawn O., 6, 86
Brakeman-Wartell, Stephanie L., 46
Brody, Gene H., 10, 53-54
Broken families, 95
Brommel, Bernard J., 10, 86
Brooks-Gunn, Jeanne, 47-48
Brotherson, Sean E., 136-137
Brown, Kathleen A., 30
Brown, Nancy Y., 91
Browning, Don, 7
Bryant, Leah, 6
Buckle, Leslie, 126
Buhrmester, Duane, 52-53
Buss, David M., 23, 45, 46
Buunk, Bram P., 45
Byfield, Link, 36
Bylund, Carma L., 10, 86
Cable, Susan M., 129
Campbell, Lori D., 127-128, 130, 132
Carnoy, Martin, 37
Carrere, Sybil, 36

Chagnon, Napoleon A., 47
Chao, Chia-Chen, 47
Charalambous, Neophytos, 56
Charmaz, Kathy, 69-70, 72
Cheadle, Jacob, 135
Cherlin, Andrew, 6, 136
Child rearing, 18, 20
Chodorow, Nancy, 34
Christakopoulou, Sophia, 55-56
Cicirelli, Victor G., 53, 56, 57
Clarke, Sally C., 12
Coan, James, 36
Cohabit, 10, 12, 37, 136
Coleman, Marilyn, 4, 8, 84, 106, 125, 129, 130
Comte, Auguste, 18, 30, 31
Connides, Ingrid Arnet, 127, 128, 130, 132
Consanguine family, 16
Consensus (solidarity), 57
Cooley, Charles Horton, 18
Coontz, Stephanie, 7, 8
Coser, Rose Laub, 20
Council on Contemporary Families, 7
Craig, Wendy M., 40-41
Crouter, Ann C., 44
Crowder, Kyle D., 8
Cumming, Edward, 55, 133
Custody, 6, 11, 12, 28
Cutrona, Carolyn E., 135
Daly, Martin, 23, 28, 39, 43, 45, 129, 130, 132
Daniels, Denise, 41
Davis, Jennifer Nerissa, 28, 45
Deal, James E., 40-41
Dey, Ian, 69, 72
Diderich, Monique, 12, 61
Differential treatment, 9, 10, 23, 39, 43-45, 47, 49, 54-55, 61
Dillman, D.A., 74
Dilution hypothesis, 44, 64, 127

Division of labor, 16, 18, 19, 28, 29, 31, 34, 37
Divorce rate, 3, 4, 9, 38
Divorce reasons, 8, 135
Doherty, William J., 7
Donovan, Josephine, 32
Dorfman, Lorraine T., 39
Drug use, 7, 135
Duberman, Lucile, 9, 132
Duncan, William C., 137
Dunn, Judy, 23, 41-42, 44, 48, 49
Durkheim, Emile, 18, 19, 56
Dworkin, Andrea, 33
Dyad, 17, 18, 21, 25, 28, 52-54, 60, 84, 85, 132
    Intergenerational, 28
    Sibling, 52-54, 60, 132
    Spousal, 17, 18, 25, 84-85
Dykstra, Pearl A., 129
Eccles, Jacquelynne S., 136
Ella Bloor, 29-31, 33
Elman, Cheryl, 20, 21, 50, 126
Emery, Robert E., 4, 9
Engels, Friedrich, 15, 16, 19
Englesson, Irmelin L., 59
Equity theory, 24, 26, 51-52
Erickson, Rosemary, 4, 6, 60
Eriksen, Shelley, 129, 130, 131
ERS Staff Report, 5, 59
Euler, Harald A., 23, 28, 46
Evolutionary theory, 28, 45-46, 56, 57, 61-63
Exchange theory, 15, 22-25, 27, 51, 52
Extended kin, 22, 42, 81, 87
Fagan, Jay, 135
Family rules, 73, 81, 86
Family systems theory, 42, 62, 84, 86
Father, 9, 12, 16, 18, 29, 32, 41, 42, 45, 46, 54, 59, 60, 63, 84, 93, 96, 115, 116, 123, 135, 136
    See also Stepfather
Fan, C. Simon, 26

Farber, Bernard, 10
Federal Interagency Forum on Child and Family Statistics, 5, 12, 88
Feinberg, Mark, 44
Feminism, 15, 29, 31-35, 66-68, 137
Festinger, Leon, 23, 49
Fields, Jason M., 4, 59
Filinson, Rachel, 39, 61
Fine, Mark, 84
Flake-Hobson, Carol, 4
Foucault, Michel, 29
Fowler, Frieda, 80
Fox, Greer L., 11, 34, 67-68
Fratricide, 55
Freud, Sigmund, 17, 48, 86
Frey, James H., 76
Friedan, Betty, 31, 35
Friedman, Debra, 27
Functional solidarity, 11-12, 57, 65, 66, 76, 102-104, 114, 115-116, 125, 129, 130, 131, 133
Furman, Wyndol, 49, 52-53
Furstenberg, Frank F., 8, 9
Gaalen, Ruben I. Van, 129
Gallagher, Maggie, 7, 36
Gallup Jr., Gordon G., 126
Galvin, Kathleen M., 10, 86
Ganong, Lawrence, 4, 8, 84, 106, 125, 129, 130
Gardels, Nathan, 35
Gaulin, Steven J. C., 46
Gay, Peter, 48
Geary, David C., 45
Gender, 11, 31, 34, 35, 36, 37, 42, 44, 51, 52, 59, 66, 68, 76, 97, 98, 106, 123, 132
Georgas, James, 55
Gerstein, Lawrence, 42
Gerth, Hans H., 19
Gerstel, Naomi, 127, 129, 130, 131
Giarrusso, Roseann, 10
Gibson, Nicole Morgan, 10
Giddens, Anthony, 19

Gilbreth, Joan G., 60
Gillis, John R., 136
Gilmore, David D., 55
Glenn, Norval, 7
Goodwin, Robin, 55-56
Gottman, John M., 36, 49
Grandfather, 46
Grandmother, 46, 119
Grandparent, 9, 46, 87, 135
Greek, April, 48
Greer, Jane, 43, 48
Grounded theory, 68-71
Group marriage, 15-16
Grumbkow, J. von, 23
Hackstaff, Karla B., 8, 31, 35-36, 89
Hagan, M.S., 41
Halverson, Charles F., 40
Hamilton, W., 28
Hammersley, Martyn, 69
Handal, Paul J., 91
Handel, Gerald, 43, 50-51, 54
Harris, Elise, 8
Hartmann, Heidi, 34
Hechter, Michael, 27
Heider, 56
Hetaerism, 16
Hetherington, E. Mavis, 7, 40, 41, 42, 44, 54, 60, 83
Hickson, David J., 26
Hinojosa, Ramon, 6, 135
Hochschild, Arlie, 9, 35, 36
Hofstede, Geert, 44
Hoier, Sabrine, 28
Homans, George C., 22, 24-25, 56
Horizontal socializing, 128
House, James, 57
Howe, G.W., 41
Hoyt, Danny R., 22, 130
Hrdy, Sara B., 46
Hyle, Patricia, 47
ICPSR, 76, 77, 78
Ihinger-Tallman, Marilyn, 4, 6, 7, 49, 79, 83, 86, 125

Inclusive fitness, 23, 28, 46-47, 57
Infanticide, 28, 39
Institute for American Values, 7, 36
Intergenerational solidarity, 56-57, 116, 127
Iulina, N.S., 33
Jankowiak, William, 11, 12, 61
Jodl, Kathleen M., 136
Johnson, David R., 135
Jones, Ann C., 40
Jorgensen, Danny L., 71-72
Keller, Heidi, 28
Kelly, John, 7
Kendrick, Carol, 49
Kerig, Patricia K., 42, 61
Kiernan, Kathleen, 136
Kiger, Gary, 35
Kin altruism, 57, 87
Kin keeper, 58, 132
King, Valerie, 42, 135
Kinship, 5, 7, 9, 20, 21, 23, 33, 50, 53, 55, 58, 81-82, 119, 130
Kinship confusion, 9
Kiselica, Mark, 42
Kivisto, Peter, 8
Knight, George P., 47
Koch, Helen L., 23
Kollock, Peter, 22
Kramer, Laurie, 49
Kreider, Rose M., 4, 59
Kurdek, Lawrence A., 84
Kurland, Jeffrey A., 45
Kurz, Demie, 7
Lalumière, Martin L., 40
Landis, K.R., 57
Lang, Frieder R., 47
Lanthier, Richard P., 49
Lasch, Christopher, 9, 21, 67
Lawton, Leora, 56
Lee, Thomas R., 132
Leigh, Geoffrey K., 132
Leon, Kim, 40
Lewin, K., 56

Lippe, Tanja Van Der, 129
Littlefield, Christine H., 46
Logan, John R., 45, 128
London, Andrew S., 20-21, 50, 126
Lüscher, Kurt, 10, 86
Lui, Hon-Kwong, 26
Luo, Ye, 7
Mabry, J. Beth, 10
Mace, Ruth, 44
MacKinnon, Carol E., 60
McBurney, Donald H., 46
McChesney, Kay Young, 56
McCoy, J. Kelly, 53-54
McGuire, Shirley, 23, 48, 49
McHale, Susan M., 44, 124
Mancini, Jay A., 132
Marshall, Catherine, 70
Marsiglio, William, 6, 135
Maternalism, 31
Matthews, Sarah H., 42
Maxwell, Joseph W., 132
Meertens, R.W., 23
Mertens, Carol E., 39
Miller, Susan J., 26
Mills, C. Wright, 19
Miner, Sonia, 39
Mother, 9, 11, 12, 15, 16, 28-35, 40, 41, 44, 45, 46, 48, 49, 54, 59, 60, 61, 82, 83, 84, 90, 96, 115, 116, 123, 124, 135, 136
  See also Stepmother
Mother-in-law, 7, 28, 119
Murray, Velma McBride, 11, 34, 67, 68
Musun-Miller, Linda, 43
Mutterrecht, 15
Myers, Edward, 43, 48
National Opinion Research Center, 77
Nepotism, 47
Normative solidarity, 11-12, 65, 76, 85, 87

Neuman, W. Lawrence, 69, 70, 72, 76
Neyer, Franz J., 47
Osgood, D. Wayne, 44
Oubaid, Viktor, 45
Pairing family, 16
Parkman, Allen M., 26
Parsons, Talcott, 21, 22, 119, 126, 127, 133
Pasley, B. Kay, 4, 7, 79, 83, 86
Paternity uncertainty, 45-46
Peterson, Richard R., 8
Pfaller, Joan, 42
Pierce, Jennifer L., 44-45
Piercy, Kathleen, 47
Plomin, Robert, 23, 41, 44, 49
Polatnitck, M. Rivka, 136
Polyandry, 16
Polygamy, 11-12, 16, 61
Poortinga, Ybe H., 55-56
Popenoe, David, 7
Previti, Denise, 135
Propinquity, 76
Proximity, 47, 56, 57, 76, 78, 112, 118, 119, 126, 132
Pulakos, Joan, 10, 58, 130
Punaluan family, 16
Quinsey, Vernon L., 40-41
Rational choice theories, 25-27, 52, 64
Reciprocal altruism, 28, 47, 57, 87
Reconstituted families, 5
Reiss, David, 41
Remarriage rate, 4, 5
Remarried families, 3-7, 9-13, 15, 25, 27, 28, 38-40, 55, 62-65, 68, 72, 73, 76, 79, 81, 83, 84, 86, 87, 88, 90, 91, 92, 96, 101, 120, 125, 130-132, 134 -136
See also Stepfamilies
Reynolds, H.T., 96
Riedmann, Agnes, 39, 58, 127
Riley, Pamela J., 35

Risch, Sharon C., 136
Rivalry, 39, 51-55, 59, 61, 62, 100, 124
Roberts, R.E.L., 11, 76
Robinson, Bryan E, 4
Rodd, Zachary A., 126
Rogers, Stacy J., 8, 56, 76
Rohde, Percy A., 28
Rosenberg, George S., 10, 58, 112
Rosenthal, Carolyn J., 132
Rossman, Gretchen B., 70
Rovine, Michael J., 41
Rubin, Beth. A., 8
Rushton, J. Philippe, 46
Salmon, Catherine A., 43, 129, 130, 132
Sanchez, Laura, 35
Sarkisian, Natalia, 127
Scanlan, James P., 33
Schlegel, Alice, 61
Schmeeckle, Maria, 132
Schneider, D.M., 55, 133
Schor, Juliet B., 32
Scott, Mindy, 135
Searight, H. Russell, 91
Shanahan, Lilly, 44
Shavitt, Yossi, 44-45
Sibship, 45, 128
Silverstein, Merrill, 10, 11, 56, 57, 76
Simmel, George, 17-18, 30, 85, 86
Simpson, Bob, 4, 9, 86
Skeen, Patsy, 4, 6, 40, 60
Skinner, B.F., 24
Smith, Dorothy, 34, 66
Smith, Trellis, 10
Social comparison, 22-24, 26, 49, 64
Social constructionist, 34
Solidarity
    Affectual, 11-12, 65, 76, 102-103, 114-117, 130, 132

Associational, 11-12, 65, 76,
  102-104, 114, 117-119, 125,
  130, 131, 133
  Consensus, 57
  Functional, 11-12, 57, 65, 66, 76,
  102-104, 114, 115, 116, 125,
  129, 130, 131, 133
  Intergenerational, 56-57, 116, 127
  Normative, 11-12, 65, 76, 85, 87
  Structural, 76
South, Scott J., 8
Spanier, Graham B., 9
Spigelman, Ami, 59
Spigelman, Gabriella, 59
Spitze, Glenda, 45, 128
SPSS, 96
Stacey, Judith, 5, 34-35
Stanley, Scott M., 7
Stepfamily, 4, 5, 7, 10, 29, 40, 60,
  73, 79, 81-86, 91, 124
  See also Remarried families
Stepfather, 6, 9, 12, 39, 40, 45, 59,
  60, 63, 134, 135, 136
Stepmother, 6, 9, 12, 74, 82, 84- 85,
  136
Stereotype, 43-44
Stocker, Clare M., 49, 124
Stoneman, Zolinda, 10, 53-54
Structural solidarity, 76
Structural-functionalists, 20-22
Sulloway, Frank J., 41-42, 47, 57
Swanson, Catherine, 36
Sweeney, Megan M., 21
Teachman, Jay, 9
Teenage pregnancies, 7
Teitler, Julien O., 8
Traditional nuclear family, 4, 7, 10,
  11, 25, 38, 39, 40, 50, 53, 61, 62,
  64, 73, 82, 84, 87-89, 97, 98, 99,
  100, 103, 104, 125, 132, 134
Trent, Katherine, 8
Triad, 18, 50, 85
Triangular families, 61

Tyron, A., 41
Uhlenberg, Peter, 39
Umberson, Debra, 57
Unclear family, 9, 86
Unspecified obligations, 24, 51, 52
U.S. Bureau of the Census, 4
United States Department of Labor,
  32
Van Der Lippe, Tanja, 129
Van Gaalen, Ruben I., 129
Voorpostel, Marieke, 125, 129
Wagner, Amy, 6, 86
Waite, Linda J., 7
Walker, Alexis, 136
Wallerstein, Judith S., 7, 135
Wampler, Karen S., 40
Weaver, Shannon E., 125, 130
Weber, Marianne, 19-20
Weber, Max, 19, 29
Weghorst, Suzanne J., 23
Weitzel, Barbara, 23, 46
White, Lynn K., 39, 56, 58, 60, 76,
  100, 127, 128
Whiteside, Mary F., 81-82
Wilson, David C., 26
Wilson, Edward Osborne, 28
Wilson, Margo, 23, 28, 39, 45
Wolff, Kurt H., 17

Monique Diderich

Dr. Monique Diderich received her Doctorate in Sociology at the University of Nevada Las Vegas. She has worked both in The Netherlands and in the United States. Dr. Diderich has taught for UNLV and for Hunter College in New York. She currently holds a position as an Assistant Professor of Sociology in the Department of Social Sciences at Shawnee State University in Portsmouth, Ohio, where she also serves as Sociology Coordinator. She publishes and teaches in the areas of marriage, family, gender, work and aging.